Understanding
DREAMS

Understanding

DREAMS

Keith Hearne & David Melbourne

NEW HOLLAND

CONTENTS

First published in 1999 by
New Holland Publishers (UK) Ltd
London • Cape Town • Sydney • Auckland

24 Nutford Place
London W1H 6DQ
United Kingdom

80 McKenzie Street
Cape Town 8001
South Africa

Level 1, Unit 4, 14 Aquatic Drive
Frenchs Forest, NSW 2086
Australia

Unit 1A
218 Lake Road
Northcote, Auckland
New Zealand

10 9 8 7 6 5 4 3 2 1

ISBN 1 85368 812 6

Editor: Alison Wormleighton
Project Art Director: Ted McCausland
Designers: Malcolm Smythe and Paul Calver
Illustrator: Jim Robins
Special Photography: HAG and Ewan Fraser
Author Photographs: Dee Johnston
Picture Researcher: Jan Croot
Jacket Design: Grahame Dudley

Editorial Direction: Yvonne McFarlane

Reproduction by
PICA Colour Separation, Singapore
Printed and bound in Singapore by
Tien Wah Press (Pte) Ltd

5

INTRODUCTION

In the last few decades, more has probably been discovered about dreams, both physiologically and psychologically, than in two millennia. As we move into the twenty-first century, it is no longer viable to regard the dream analysts Sigmund Freud and Carl Jung as having the topic "all sewn up." In fact, nothing could be further from the truth.

Certainly these individuals made some valuable contributions to our understanding of sleep and dreams. However, in the late nineteeth/early twentieth centuries, when Freud and Jung were devising their theories, dream analysts had only limited access to dream accounts, and there was no knowledge of the physiology of sleep and dreaming or of the way dreams are structured by the brain. No doubt if Freud and Jung could have availed themselves of modern technology and methods, they would have abandoned many of their own hypotheses.

Today, more and more exciting discoveries are being made on a regular basis, with the advent of sleep laboratories, in which scientific monitoring of sleep and dreaming takes place; through the use of computers, which allow sophisticated analysis of the data; and through the vast numbers of dream accounts that the authors obtain through the media and on the Internet.

Freud barely paid lip service to the important subject of "lucid" dreaming, in which the dreamer is conscious that he or she is dreaming. Indeed, in order to make this remarkable dreaming condition fit in with his theories, he even suggested that being conscious within a dream represented wish fulfilment, in that the dreamer was striving for the ultimate dream experience. Clearly, his understanding of lucid dreams was very limited.

In fact, lucid dreaming is one of the main areas to have advanced our understanding of the nature of dreams. Research on lucid dreaming, together with sleep-laboratory investigations, has enabled us to enter the dream objectively and inspect its workings.

Before we, the authors of this book, joined forces in dream research, many of our theories were running in parallel. When we did come together, in 1994, the advantages were apparent right from the outset — we found that we were constantly sparking off each other in developing new ideas and techniques for various dream-research projects. It was as if we had opened a new door of discovery.

As we continually bounced ideas off each other in the field of dream interpretation, we perceived something of a paradox. We realized that, in many respects, ancient civilizations – unrestricted by the sceptical strait-jacket of behaviourist science – appeared to have a far better understanding of dreams than modern man. Moreover, diverse cultures which are scattered throughout the world today, such as those of the Aboriginal Australians, Native Americans and West Indians, as well as many African civilizations, have a better understanding than the west of certain aspects of dreaming, particularly the spiritual dimension.

We discovered that by keeping in mind all theories about dreaming, both past and present, much deeper insights into the mysterious world of dreams were forthcoming. Similarly, we found that far more sense could be made of dreams if we took into account such factors as the existence of the soul, various paranormal events like premonitions and telepathy, and other related occurrences.

The world of dreams does not recognize the constraints of the laws of physics, so why are they constantly applied to a dimension where anything is possible? For example, modern scientists refuse to accept the possibility of premonitions. They maintain that it is impossible to experience an effect before the cause, therefore foreknowledge simply cannot exist. Yet if you ask a friend or family member if they have ever had a premonition or know somebody who has, the answer is likely to be in the affirmative. Dreams are a common vehicle for accurate premonitions (known as precognitive dreams), and, as we will see later in this book, more and more of these are being reported.

Ultimately, sleep-laboratory work is limited to providing data. Real inroads are made, however, when somebody follows a hunch or, employing a little lateral thinking, pursues ideas modern science might not countenance. Indeed, had it not been for Dr. Hearne following a hunch, structured communication from a lucid dreamer to the outside world might never have been established. David Melbourne's theory of the "trigger mechanism" in sleep that identifies message-bearing dreams (whereby the unconscious actually awakens the dreamer to force attention on the dream) would probably have gone undiscovered for years.

We both recognized that for an analyst to decode a dream's message accurately, they must first learn all

there is to learn about sleep and, in particular, dreams. It is necessary to consider ancient as well as modern theories concerning this vast subject. When they are blended with the ideas of different cultures from around the world and added to modern scientific investigations, a clearer, more complete picture begins to emerge. This ongoing research and refusal to be bound by the dogmatic constraints of science has lead to many fascinating discoveries, which are outlined in this book.

In the first chapter we examine the background to the subject, including the beliefs of ancient civilizations and modern cultures, important dreams through history, major theories about dreaming such as those of Freud and Jung as well as modern theories, significant recent research and data on animals' sleeping experiences.

The second chapter explains the phenomena of sleep and dreaming, including the basic sleep cycles and how a dream is structured. It also covers imagery that may occur as a person is drifting off to sleep (known as hypnagogic imagery) and as they are waking up (hypnopompic imagery), all of which can be put to constructive uses such as problem-solving.

Precognition, dream telepathy and other related paranormal phenomena are also examined in this chapter. We look at the sometimes terrifying condition known as sleep paralysis, and establish how this could be confused with accounts of alien abductions, apparitions or sensing the presence of somebody who has malicious intent.

In the third chapter we look at sleep disorders, such as insomnia, sleepwalking and sleep-talking, teeth-grinding, bedwetting, night terrors and snoring. Many of the problems described here can be alleviated or cured with straightforward therapy techniques, and these are included at the end of this chapter, along with the "scripts" that are used to deal with each problem.

The elimination of nightmares is a priority subject and is examined in detail here. At least a million people in Britain are estimated to suffer two or more nightmares a week. Quadruple the number of sufferers for the United States, and increase it proportionately for countries with higher populations, and the size of the problem on a world-wide scale becomes apparent. We have developed techniques to deal with nightmares, and these are explained in this chapter.

Lucid dreaming is dealt with in the fourth chapter. We look at ways in which this amazing dream state could be used to initiate precognitive dreams, administer healing, lower stress levels, enhance creativity and fulfil other constructive applications. We also examine how lucid dreaming can have such a powerful effect on people that it changes their perspective on life itself. Included here are techniques for using "scripts" to induce a lucid dream and to convert a nightmare into a lucid dream.

False awakenings are another fascinating dream state covered in this chapter. These provide the dream enthusiast with an opportunity to initiate lucid

dreams, conduct experiments to discover more consistent effects, and perhaps even carry out research into the paranormal! Also covered in the fourth chapter are other topics on the frontiers of current dream research, including hypno-oneirography, a tracing technique for viewing mental imagery from hypnotically induced dreams.

A link is established between nightmares and neurological visions created by the subconscious following trauma. We investigate how these sometimes disturbing visions can be transformed into more

pleasant experiences by employing a method used to eradicate nightmares, thus eliminating the need for medicinal drugs.

Finally, in the fifth chapter, we look at means by which you can delve deeper into particularly significant dreams and begin to explore their meanings. Hidden in the enigmatic world of dreams is a realm of magic and seemingly unlimited knowledge

and wisdom. As everyone spends approximately six years of their life dreaming, it makes sense to develop an understanding of this inner universe, in order to access these mysteries and truths. Exploring dreams can often lead to far greater insights into the dreamer's own life.

APPROACHES TO DREAMING

Dreams have fascinated mankind from time immemorial. The ancients believed that dreams were messages from the gods, and recognized that they were capable of foretelling the future, shedding light on the past and present, and altering people's lives. Some dreams have even changed history. Science has made progress in understanding the processes of sleep and dreaming, yet there is still much that can be learned from the ancients, and from the cultures scattered around the world today who have

not lost touch with their ancestors' understanding of dreams. What is needed is a synthesis of the old wisdom and the new discoveries if we are to understand and benefit from dreaming.

DREAMS IN ANCIENT CIVILIZATIONS

It is likely that in early societies, unencumbered by the multitude of distractions that affect people today, many important truths about dreams were discovered. Among the deities worshipped by these societies were gods and goddesses of dreams, reflecting the significance with which dreaming was regarded.

Babylonia, Assyria and Egypt

References to the meanings of specific dreams were found in some of the earliest surviving writings of the human race – clay tablets bearing cuneiform script, from Babylonia and Assyria, found at the site of the great library at Nineveh. And one of the Babylonian deities for whom temples were built was Mamu, the goddess of dreams.

ABOVE In ancient Egypt, statues of sphinxes, such as this ivory one, represented the king or a god. In about 1450 BC the future King Thutmose IV had a prophetic dream in which he was promised the throne if he would clear away the sand engulfing a sphinx.

ABOVE Examples of man's earliest known writing – the cuneiform script on clay tablets similar to this one from Babylonia – contained references to dream meanings.

The ancient Egyptians paid much attention to their dreams. In temples known as serapeums (named after the god of dreams, Serapis) dream "incubation" was practised. The intensely ritualistic procedure was intended to encourage an especially informative dream that originated from the gods and would be interpreted by the oracles or "learned men of the magic library."

The person undergoing the dream incubation, called the incubant, would sleep at the temple after having taken part, perhaps for several days, in various rituals of cleansing, fasting, abstaining from sex, making offerings and praying. Sometimes harmless snakes were placed near the bed. All these unusual situations probably put the incubant in a suitably expectant frame of mind for a meaningful dream. It appears that dreams could also be incubated through the use of a "stand-in."

Incubation seems to have been enormously popular and effective – major dream temples existed at Thebes and Memphis in Egypt and at many other sites in the Near East. Incubated dreams were used for a variety of purposes, including to discover the appropriate herbal remedy or other cure for an illness, to obtain guidance on topics such as what to do about a relationship and to predict the future.

One prophetic dream that apparently did not require incubation was the dream of Prince Thutmose, later Thutmose IV of Egypt (c.1450 BC). Visitors to the great sphinx at Giza today can see an inscription he placed on it recording that, while asleep by the sphinx, he was promised the kingdom by the god Hormakhu in return for clearing away the sand from the statue.

Some ancient Egyptian papyri provide lists of dream themes and their meanings. One such document, from the 13th dynasty (1770 BC) states that if a woman dreams of kissing her husband, trouble lies ahead. This is an example of an "opposite" – a notion that often crops up in dream interpretation everywhere – in which the dream means the reverse of what it appears to mean.

Greece

The ancient Greeks believed dreams were caused by the gods communicating with people through Hypnos and Morpheus, the gods of sleep and dreams. It was thought that a god or a ghost would visit the dreamer, entering the room through a keyhole.

As in Egypt, dream incubation was widely practised in Greece, especially for acquiring useful information that would bring about a cure for an illness. At Oropos and Epidaurus there were famous sleep temples dedicated to Asklepios, the god of medicine. The dreams that people experienced while sleeping there were interpreted by physician-priests.

We don't really know how effective dream incubation was, but it was used for thousands of years and many grateful incubants left testimonials inscribed on the walls of temples. Various forms of trickery may have been involved, such as voice production and the surreptitious administration of drugs but, equally, the strong anticipation built up in the incubant was probably enough to initiate the necessary dream.

The seminal *Treatise on Dreams*, attributed to the Greek physician Hippocrates (c.460–c.377 BC), the "father of medicine," asserted that dreams could indicate imminent disease by way of symbolism. A dream of seeing bright stars would indicate a healthy body, whereas observing dim stars preceded illness. A dream of rivers pointed to an excess of blood. Thus, the microcosm of the body's state of health was associated with the macrocosm of the universe. While Hippocrates accepted that some dreams were "divine," the Greek philosopher and scientist Aristotle (384–322 BC) refuted the notion. In his work *On Sleep and Waking*, he pointed out that if the gods sent dreams, then only intelligent and learned people should receive them, which obviously was not the case, and that even lowly animals dream. Aristotle also noted that dreams could be influenced by internal stimuli. Another Greek philosopher, Plato (c.427–347 BC), wrote that we possess "a lawless wild beast nature which peers out in sleep."

ABOVE The ruins of the snake-pit in the ancient Greek sleep temple at Epidaurus, where snake-healing as well as dream incubation was practised.

In ancient Greece, as in China and several other ancient societies, the soul was considered to travel about during sleep. The Greeks told of an astral-travelling type of phenomenon experienced frequently by one Hermotimus of Clazomenae. He would visit various places in sleep and report back what he saw. However, one night when he was "out," his enemies burnt his "deserted" body.

Rome

Roman beliefs about dreams were similar to those of ancient Greece. Their premonitory aspect was taken seriously. The historian Plutarch (c.AD 45-125) mentioned that Calpurnia, the wife of Julius Caesar (100–44 BC), dreamed of his assassination the night before it occurred. Caesar's adopted heir, the emperor Augustus (63 BC–AD 14), actually made a law that in parts of the Roman Empire anyone having a dream about the empire's welfare had to announce the dream in a market-place.

ABOVE Vincenzo Camuccini's painting The Death of Julius Caesar. *Caesar's wife is said to have dreamed of his assassination the previous night.*

It is reported that the day before the tyrannical and mad Roman emperor Caligula was assassinated, in AD 41, he had a dream in which he was standing by the heavenly throne of Jupiter. The god gave him a push with the big toe of his right foot, causing Caligula to tumble to earth.

An outstanding legacy of Roman dream interpretation is the five-volume *Oneirocritica* ("The Interpretation of Dreams"), compiled by Artemidorus of Daldis (c.AD 200). Drawing on much earlier information, it includes over three thousand dream reports, from all sorts of people and walks of life.

The *Oneirocritica* divides dreams into two broad classes: Insomnium, about everyday things, and Somnium, concerning the future. The approach was systematic, with an initial decision as to whether the events were natural, lawful, customary for the dreamer, and so on. It was clearly understood that each dream was individual to the dreamer.

However, verbal puns were recognized and some symbolism identified. Ploughing the ground, for example, was known to be a sexual symbol. Dreaming about one's mouth might represent home, with the teeth symbolizing the people in the home. Much accumulated knowledge was crystallized in those major, insightful volumes.

India

An ancient Indian book of Hindu wisdom – the *Atharva Veda* (written around 1500–1000 BC) – comments that being passive in a dream, or suffering some kind of loss in one, was a bad omen, whereas an aggressive dream was favourable, even if the dreamer suffered mutilation in it. It advised that if a series of dreams from one night were recalled, only the last should be interpreted, since a refining process was operating during sleep until an appropriate conclusion was reached. For the first time, the dreamer's personality type (phlegmatic, sanguine or bilious) was taken into account in dream interpretation.

Regarding dreams of the future, it was stated that the later in the night the dream happened, the sooner the actual event would occur. Presumably, much observation had been conducted on forewarning dreams to come to that conclusion and for it to be stated as wisdom.

The Far East

The ancient Buddhist *Tibetan Book of the Dead* basically sees death as a dreamlike condition. The book, which was ritualistically read to the deceased, describes three distinct illusory states (Chikai, Chonyid and Sidpa) which generate visions, both pleasant and fearful, based on the individual's expectations. It says that if at any time the individual can recognize the situation as being unreal (like becoming "lucid," which involves becoming aware of being in an ongoing nocturnal dream, as explained on page 33), the soul elevates to a higher plane and so avoids the constant cycle of death and rebirth.

One important Taoist manuscript, the *Lie-tseu*, listed six different types of dream: ordinary dreams, terror dreams, day-residue dreams, dreams of waking, joyful dreams and dreams of fear.

The Chinese knew that external stimuli could be incorporated into dreams, so that if a person slept on a belt, for example, a snake might be dreamed of. Singing and dancing meant imminent weeping — again, this involves the concept of opposites (see page 15).

In China (as well as Greece and several other ancient societies) the person's soul, or intrinsic awareness, was considered to travel about during sleep. Dream experiences were taken to be indistinguishable from those of wakefulness.

Some stories (for instance, of flying) told by people from isolated cultures in the Far East probably sounded to Westerners like lies — but they were true accounts reported by people who genuinely recognized no boundary between dreams and wakefulness. In those cultures, the absence of the soul was supposed to leave the sleeper vulnerable. If the soul did not

LEFT In ancient Tibet it was believed that the interval between death and rebirth was spent in a dreamlike state, encountering frightening apparitions derived from the person's expectations. In this traditional Tibetan tanka, *the demon Mara, the Tempter, is shown grasping the Wheel of Life.*

return, the body would die. The soul could meet with an accident, or it might have been deliberately trapped. For instance, the sorcerers of the Danger Islands in the Pacific would set up snares, of various sizes, for human souls that might come by.

A sleeper's appearance was not to be altered by, say, painting a moustache on a woman while she slept, because the returning soul would not recognize her and she would die. Also, a sleeping person had never to be woken suddenly, because the soul needed time to rush back to the body.

BELOW A relief carving from the great pyramid at the ancient Mayan city of Chichen Itza. The Mayans had great esteem for individuals who were able to predict the future through the interpretation of dreamlike visions.

Central America

In Central America's pre-Mayan and Mayan cultures, divination included producing dreams and visions (involving the same visual-imaging process). Those who divined were highly respected in such societies because they steered the nation through natural disasters and other dangers and vicissitudes. Several methods were employed to induce visions including fasting, loss of sleep and chewing coca leaves. One method was to kill an animal, wrap its skin around the diviner's neck and half strangle the person until loss of consciousness resulted and imagery was produced.

Young people entering puberty underwent fasting as part of an initiatory process. Dreams that occurred during that time were interpreted and were supposed to illustrate the whole future life of the person.

RELIGIOUS DREAMS

Dreams were of great importance in the history and holy books of the world's religions.

Buddhism

Highly symbolic dreams were reported relating to the life of Gautama Buddha (c.563–c.483 BC). His mother dreamed of being pregnant with an elephant which was shining silvery-white and possessed six tusks. For a long time it had been predicted that a chosen one would arrive, and this dream was seen by the interpreters as an announcement of the arrival.

Gautama's father, a raja (noble), experienced a dream of his son leaving the family and becoming a monk; and Gautama's wife saw herself in a dream naked, with hands and feet amputated, and viewing various catastrophic scenes. Gautama interpreted this as representing him leaving her and the family in order to seek enlightenment, which he did at the age of about 30, when he became an ascetic.

Christianity

The Christian Bible relates several accounts of dreams as divine revelations. In the Old Testament many dreams are mentioned, often coinciding with critical times in the development of Judaism. Dreams could recur until appropriate action was taken.

Such a case was that of the two dreams of the Egyptian Pharaoh who dreamed that seven fat cattle were eaten by seven skeletal ones, and then that seven ripe ears of corn on a stalk were swallowed up by seven thin, blighted ears (Genesis 41).

The puzzling dreams were deciphered by Joseph, who had already demonstrated some skill at interpreting dreams. Joseph recognized them as

LEFT An eighteenth-century Tibetan painting depicting Buddha cutting his hair in preparation for renouncing the world — an event about which both his wife and his father had dreamed.

would save his people from their sins; the next told them to flee to Egypt, as Herod planned to kill the child; the third informed them of Herod's death; and another told them to move to Galilee.

For a few hundred years after the death of Christ, Christian writers commented on dreams. St. Augustine (354–430), the greatest of the Latin Church Fathers, believed that dreams could be influenced by demons. The theologian Gregory of Nyssa (c.331–95) wrote that an individual's nature was revealed in his dreams. However, in the Middle Ages, any interest in dreams was seriously curtailed when the subject was linked with sorcery.

ABOVE In the Bible, Joseph was a skilled interpreter of dreams. Stages in his life are depicted in this nineteenth-century stained glass window at Lincoln Cathedral, England.

dreams of the future. He knew that the fact that the dreams had come to a Pharaoh pointed to a major, national matter, and he realized that both dreams meant the same thing. Joseph saw the dreams as illustrating seven years of plentiful harvest, followed by seven years of little or no harvest, which would destroy the benefit of the good years. The Pharaoh acted on the interpretation and set about building up large stores of grain. The interpretation apparently saved the country and the ruling system.

In the New Testament, four dreams of an important nature happened to Mary's husband, Joseph (Matthew 1–2). The first encouraged him to accept her pregnancy and to name the baby Jesus, because he

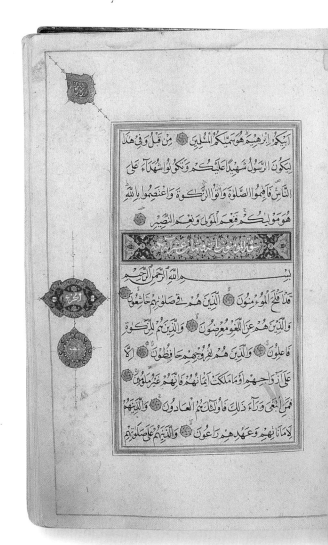

Islam

Dreams seem to have been of some consequence in the building of Islam. The archangel Gabriel is said to have appeared to Muhammad, the founder of the religion, and dictated the first chapter, or Sura, of the Koran, the holy book of Islam. The adhan, or call to prayers by the muezzin from a minaret, was dreamed about by one of Muhammad's disciples and subsequently incorporated into the daily prayer ritual. In 620, Muhammad experienced a dream or vision

BELOW The Sura, the first chapter of the Koran — the holy book of Islam — was dictated to Muhammad by the archangel Gabriel during a vision.

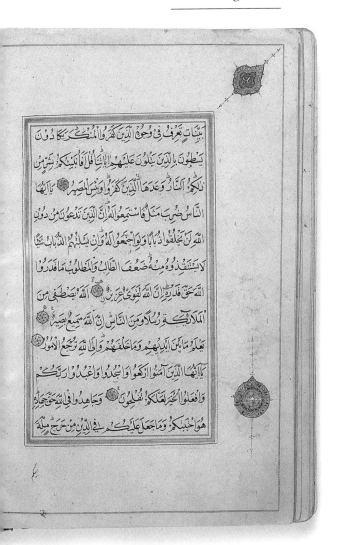

ABOVE Muhammad's dream of his Night Journey with the archangel Gabriel has inspired many paintings.

that he journeyed in the company of the archangel Gabriel and angels. He travelled on a strange creature called a buraq and was taken to holy places and to the seven levels of heaven and hell, and he met significant religious leaders and prophets from the past. This famous experience of Muhammad, termed the Night Journey, has inspired many poets and artists.

BELIEFS OF OTHER CULTURES

Anthropological investigations have thrown light on similarities and differences between cultures in their beliefs about dreams. Dreams relate to the way of life

of each group: animals figure prominently in the
dreams of hunting cultures, fish in those of oceanic
peoples, and so on. In all these cultures, dreams are
respected as coming from a revered source and holding
key knowledge that can assist the dreamer. Dreams
that describe the future are fully accepted.

Interpreting signs

In Trinidad, the belief has been that dreams are
communications from the spirit realm and so contain
important news. Certain signs have been accepted
from dreams. Thus, persons seen flying in dreams will
succeed; the presence of a large black snake urges the
dreamer to beware the approach of an enemy; seeing a
policeman foretells a court appearance. Perhaps based
on the trading history of the place, a boat seen
moving away is interpreted as inauspicious, because
something is going from the dreamer, whereas a vessel
that is approaching is deciphered as bringing good
news. A common belief in the West Indies is that to
dream of fish means pregnancy.

The Pagiboti people of Zaire consider that dreams
are sent from their ancestors. The Pagiboti are hunters
as well as horticulturists. Hunting is important to
their survival, and their dreams sometimes give
information on future success or otherwise. For
instance, a dream of encountering an animal in the
forest is a good sign.

For the indigenous Malays, to dream of a gale in
early morning refers to sorrow; hail means acquiring
property; bathing in rain portends escape from great
danger; mosquitoes mean an enemy is approaching.

Native American dream catchers

In Native American culture, dreams are believed to
descend from the night sky, as messages from sacred
spirits. To filter out the bad dreams and allow only
good dreams to reach the sleeping person, a "dream
catcher" is suspended near the sleeper. This device
consists of a cobweb-like structure on a circular frame,

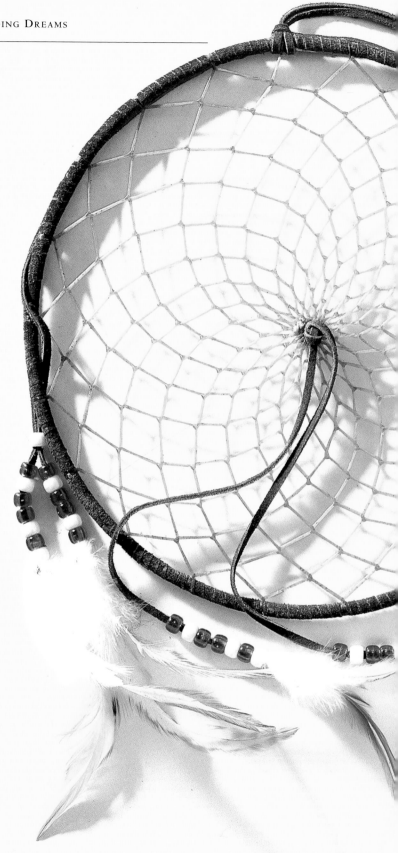

LEFT Native American dream catchers are said to prevent bad dreams from reaching people sleeping near them.

with feathers attached. The web snares the bad dreams, which will disappear in the morning sun. Pleasant dreams pass through the centre hole of the dream catcher to reach the individual; these will be fulfilled in the sleeper's destiny. The web represents the web of life, and dream catchers are Native American symbols of good luck.

Aboriginal Australian Dreamtime

In the Aboriginal Australian scheme of things, the earth was formed and beings created during an ancient yet timeless mythological era called Dreamtime or The Dreaming. It was the era of creation of life-forms, and the establishment of society's laws and rituals. The Aboriginal legends, rich in symbolism, describe how the Powers — great spirits emerging from the earth, sea and sky — took on various forms, particularly of animals, and moved over the world.

RIGHT Aboriginal paintings from Australia's Northern Territory. The Aboriginal Australians believe that the Powers took on the form of animals, and that each Aboriginal has an ancestor linked to a particular animal.

They shaped mountain ranges and other geographical features and began the plan of life which the Aboriginals try to follow in their daily lives. Each Aboriginal has a personal Dreamtime forebear, linked to a specific animal.

DREAMS THAT CHANGED HISTORY

Various tales have come down from the past about dreams that changed the course of history. Alexander the Great, while involved in the rather drawn-out siege of Tyros in 332 BC, dreamed of a satyr (the word is "satyros" in Greek) – a Greek woodland god with a horse's ears and tail – dancing on a shield. His dream-interpreters noticed that it was a phonetic dream – the letters of satyros could be split to make Sa Tyros, meaning "Tyros is thine." Alexander was influenced by the dream to continue the siege, and was victorious.

In 49 BC, in defiance of the Roman senate and armies, Julius Caesar decided to march across the Rubicon (the river forming the boundary of his province) to attack Rome. His decision was said to have been made after he dreamed of incest with his mother, which was interpreted as symbolizing territorial conquest. The phrase "crossing the Rubicon," meaning taking a decisive and irrevocable step, comes from this decision. (Caesar was vindicated, as he was not only victorious but within three months was master of all Italy.)

Adolf Hitler, when he was a 28-year-old non-commissioned officer in the First World War, apparently dreamed he was buried by a shell. It was the long Battle of the Somme, and all was quiet at the time. Disturbed by the clarity of the dream, he left the bunker and wandered into "no man's land" – which was dangerous. Suddenly, a shell hit the place where he had been sleeping, killing all his comrades. This dream, and his fortuitous avoidance of death, may have convinced the future führer that he was especially protected and chosen for a major political role.

LEARN HOW TO DREAM

In 1865 a dream about a snake with its tail in its mouth led to the discovery of the ring structure of the benzene molecule, which revolutionized organic chemistry.

Afterwards, its discoverer, the German chemist F. A. Kekulé von Stradonitz, announced to colleagues, "Gentlemen, we must learn how to dream." However, he was not alone in his enthusiasm. Throughout history people have suspected that limitless wisdom and knowledge could be accessed in the inner universe of dreams.

At about the time of Kekulé von Stradonitz's discovery, the Russian chemist Dmitri Mendeleyev had been speculating about ways in which new chemical elements could be recognized. Having decided to sleep on the problem, he dreamt of a table on to which elements fell in the correct order. Upon waking, he set about devising the periodic table of elements, which became the central concept of modern inorganic chemistry. From this Mendeleyev was able to predict the existence of several previously undiscovered elements.

Yet another mid-nineteenth century breakthrough, the lock-stitch sewing machine, might not have been a part of our everyday lives had it not been for a dream by the American inventor Elias Howe. He dreamt that he was being held captive by a tribe of barbarous warriors, who were intending to run him through with spears. In his fear, his thoughts naturally focused on the threatening spear tips, which, he noticed, each housed a small eye-shaped hole. Immediately upon waking

BELOW Until around the nineteenth century, dreams were associated with sorcery. Occult tradition held that nightmares came from demons such as the incubus and succubus, which attacked the sleeper sexually. An incubus is depicted in the late eighteenth-century painting The Nightmare, *by Henry Fuseli.*

from his dream, Howe knew that he had found the key to mechanized sewing: a needle which had a hole near the point.

NINETEENTH-CENTURY INSIGHTS INTO DREAMS

The medieval Church's linkage of dream divination with sorcery led to a long hiatus in the interest in dreams. It was not broken until the nineteenth century when, in the new age of reason, some scientists again looked into sleep and dreaming.

Various observations provided many new insights into the dream state. With regard to the question of where the "building material" of dreams comes from, it was realized that some of it derives from forgotten or faint memories. In 1885 the Frenchman Delboeuf traced back the name of a plant that came up in a dream to two years previously, when he had written it in a book. Another Frenchman, Alfred Maury, in 1878 saw a man who gave his name in a dream — discovering later that he had known the man as a child. Recent memories, especially of the day before, appearing in dreams became known as *day residues*.

To many nineteenth-century dream researchers it was obvious that dreams follow associative pathways, and Maury gave examples of phonetic links.

According to research by Maury and the Marquis Hervey de St. Denys (see page 33), external stimuli, such as noises and scents, register in dreams and can be incorporated into them. It was also known that internal stimuli, such as ringing in the ears, can influence content, so the mind becomes more aware of the body — as Aristotle had long ago stated.

Certain dreams were given a physiological explanation. Thus, the dream of flying was supposed to be caused by the sensation of the lungs sinking when the thorax (chest) was insensitive during sleep.

One far-reaching feature of dreaming was noticed by the German theologian, Friedrich Schleiermacher, who pointed out in 1862 that when awake we think in ideas, but in sleep we think in pictures. This transformation of an idea into a hallucination was termed *dramatization* by Hans Spitta, the German philosopher, in 1892. The extraordinary out-of-character behaviour of people in dreams was commented on in 1856 by Jessen, who pointed out the seeming lack of conscience: when dreaming, a person may think nothing of murder. It seemed to Hildebrandt in 1875 that this is due to the removal of inhibition in sleep, so that one's basic nature reveals itself.

It was generally accepted by the late nineteenth century that dreams were associated with a partial waking state. In 1878, Binz, a German thinker, declared that sleep was due to "fatigued albumen in the brain" and dreams happened when some slight consciousness returned.

The idea that dreams gave the mind a playground to provide intellectual recreation during sleep was proposed by Yves Burdach in 1830. In 1861, the French philosopher Delage suggested the notion that dreams resolved psychic tensions caused by the repression of material. Also that year Albert Scherner suggested that decentralization occurs in sleep, so that fantasy takes over, and thoughts are dramatized into pictures. He was aware of sexual symbolism; so, for example, the penis might be represented by a clarinet, pubic hair by fur, female thighs by a narrow courtyard, and the vagina by a slippery path.

FREUD'S THEORIES

Scherner could not propose a useful function for dreams – but the Austrian neurologist Sigmund Freud (1856–1939) could. Freud built an elaborate and controversial scheme of things on his, and others', ideas.

Sigmund Freud established the basic method of psychoanalysis, "free association," whereby the patient reports any thoughts or images evoked by a word. A bold pioneer, he, in effect, "discovered" the unconscious, and his views were highly influential in western science, art and culture. His major work,

The Interpretation of Dreams, was published in 1900. To Freud, the dream was the "royal road to the knowledge of the unconscious in mental life."

Freud's assessment of dreams involved his concept of the personality as consisting of three components: the *id*, a primitive, selfish part continually demanding gratification of basic urges centred on sex and aggression (rather like Plato's "wild beast" – see page 15); the *ego*, interacting with the real world and aware of what is possible; and the *super-ego*, which reminds the individual of moral and ethical considerations – usually reflecting parental influences.

In the dream, with the conscious ego absent, the id's incessant demands result in an appropriate visual pandering to the underlying urge. But in order not to offend the super-ego, those unacceptable thoughts are changed – by a process of subterfuge known as the *dream work* – to thoughts that are acceptable.

An internal censor is cunningly evaded by producing symbolic versions of the "unacceptable" thoughts: the initial *latent content* (the thoughts of the id) is transformed into the *manifest content* (the dream). Incorporating Spitta's notion of dramatization (see page 27), Freud said that thoughts are linked, giving rise to something like a theatrical production.

Disguise techniques

Various "disguise" techniques were described by Freud. In *condensation*, different wishes fuse pictorial symbols together, thus producing unusual and often impossible images – a dream person might have features of several other individuals. The

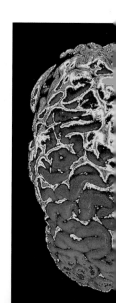

RIGHT The brain viewed from the top, showing the left and right sides. Dreaming is likely to be a normal function of the right side, which controls mental imagery. This contradicts Freud's theory that dreams are devised by the mind to disguise distasteful wishes.

important interpretational point is what links the different components. For example, a person in a dream might have the face of one friend but the hair style of another, which might constitute a wish for one of them to be like the other.

A favourite method of disguise is to introduce *opposites*, a phenomenon the ancient Egyptians and Chinese were familiar with thousands of years ago (see page 15). A dream of a funeral, for instance, may express a birth wish.

Another disguise technique is *transference* — displacing the main element on to a seemingly unimportant feature. The appearance in dreams of bizarre sequences of images seemed to be explained by the repertoire of disguises suggested by Freud.

Repressed wishes behind dreams

Another centrepoint of Freud's theory was that the organism basically seeks inactivity, and so the purpose of a dream is, in a sense, to pander to and placate the troublesome id. By providing gratification, however illusory, the indirect yet main consequence is that the individual stays asleep. The dream "guards" sleep and so, essentially, the source of each dream is an unacceptable, disguised wish. The interpretation of dreams, according to Freud, involves tracing the antecedents by the process of free association and eventually coming up with the repressed root wishes.

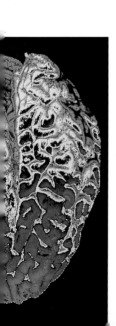

We can understand why Freud made these assumptions. It has always been common knowledge that men have erections while dreaming, even though the dream content may be totally non-sexual, and we know that dreams produce sexual symbolism. Introducing symbolism in order to evade some part of the mind that would find the sexual material distasteful initially seems perfectly plausible. Freud's approach was superficially compelling and fascinating,

ABOVE *Freud's patients would relax on this couch during therapy exploring the unconscious. Freud sat behind them.*

providing an overall structure that fitted in with many observations about dreams. A modern perspective, however, reveals major weaknesses.

Flaws in the theory

Crucial to Freud's theory is that dreams disguise — but is that actually the case? Dream symbols might not be deliberately devious disguises but simply expressive devices that occur also in waking life.

The brain consists of a right side and a left side. It is generally accepted today that the left side of the brain is associated with logic, reason and language whereas the right side is more to do with imagery and creativity. In view of these differences, it is more probable that dreaming is simply associated with activity on the right side of the brain, where verbalization is transformed into visualization.

Nightmares could not be comfortably embraced by Freud's notions. What could be the wish behind a dream that is so fearful it awakens the dreamer? Freud thought that perhaps the dream work had been incompetent so that direct wishes inadvertently presented themselves, or that the fulfilment of the wish itself raised too much anxiety.

In addition, the apparent link between erections and dreams, which was thought to support Freud's sexual basis of dreams, has been found to be spurious. In sleep-laboratory studies carried out in the US in 1965 by Ismet Karacan and colleagues, it was found that if subjects were woken each time they entered dreaming sleep, eventually the cycle of erections would shift out of phase with the cycle of dreaming periods. So it seems that the penile arousal cycle is actually independent of dreaming sleep despite the fact that it normally coincides with it.

Freud's theories are a provocative viewpoint which may or may not contain certain truths. Other theorists have presented equally plausible accounts of what happens when we dream.

JUNG'S THEORIES

The main challenger to Freud's concepts was the Swiss psychiatrist Carl Jung (1875–1961), the founder of "analytical psychology." Jung was initially one of Freud's followers, but he broke away in 1913. One reason was his inability to accept Freud's dogma about the sexual basis of behaviour and dreams.

Jung saw the psyche as self-adjusting so that in life we can reconcile opposing parts of our nature. The unconscious is not just a storehouse of repressed wishes – it also acts as friend, guide and adviser.

Dreams, according to Jung, have a special compensatory function, alerting us to imbalances in our personality and enabling us to alter our behaviour. For example, a tendency towards arrogance might be countered, perhaps, by a "reductive" dream in which we are humbled in some way.

He saw the dream as a means of communication, to bring unconscious information to conscious awareness. The Jungian analyst uses direct associations to keep the patient focused on the dream, rather than leading away from it by free association. The dream, as seen by Jung, also looks forward to future possibilities

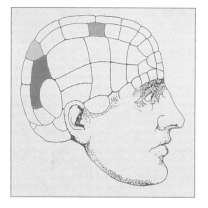

ABOVE Nineteenth-century phrenological charts illustrated the areas of the brain that were thought to control specific faculties. Theories at this time to account for sleep and dreaming included "fatigued albumen in the brain" and the need to "excrete useless ideas."

– a concept very different from the backward-looking perspective Freud perceived in dreams.

In Jung's view, some dreams touch on a "collective unconscious," the elements in everyone's unconscious that derive from the experiences of all mankind. There are universal archetypal images which appear in dreams and have a common significance – such as the anima (feminine part of a man's personality) and animus (masculine part of a woman's personality), the wise old man, and the earth mother. The Jungian approach is spiritual and positive, stressing how dreams can help each of us in our personal self-development.

MODERN THEORIES OF DREAMING

Like Jung, the Austrian psychiatrist Alfred Adler (1870–1937) veered away from Freud. The main difference between Freud's and Adler's approaches was that Adler did not see much divergence between a person's thoughts during wakefulness and those in sleep. Freud's theory of an elaborate disguise mechanism was not accepted by him. However, Adler did agree that dreams centre on unresolved matters in the dreamer's life.

Montague Ullman, of the Maimonides Medical Center in New York, supported Jung rather than Freud. In 1958 and 1962 he stressed the dream's capacity for revelation rather than concealment. He, too, appreciated the metaphorical aspect of dreams.

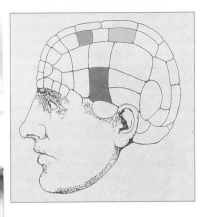
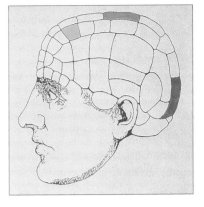

Some therapists today who are attached to the Freudian viewpoint will still look for sexual wishes in dreams, and Jungian enthusiasts will seek mandalas (certain symbols) and archetypes. But a more eclectic approach has generally become established in dream interpretation. In modern writings, dogmatic assertions have been abandoned and a mixture of techniques and beliefs is being employed. For example, the English dreams researcher Ann Faraday encourages the recording of a dream diary and a "discussion," when awake, between the dreamer and any dream character, to determine more about the character. (This method was also developed by the psychologist Fritz Perls – see page 123.)

Faraday urges the dreamer to take the dream literally – it might be a reminder or warning. The dream should be read as a metaphor, and the feelings experienced during the dream give a clue as to the problem it touches on. The dream points to something that needs attention and the interpretation will be recognized when it is correct. Faraday tells the dreamer to look out for puns, whether verbal, metaphorical or literal.

OTHER CONTRIBUTIONS

Discoveries and technical developments in areas other than psychology have resulted in further speculations about dreams. In 1964, Evans and Newman, using the analogy with the then recently introduced computer, observed that the machines were taken off-line from time to time to update programs and remove excess

data. Perhaps, they suggested, such intervals of closure corresponded to the periods of dreaming sleep and dreams were simply by-products of the process.

Analogous thinking, though, can sometimes create inappropriate concepts when applied to a different area. The human brain, which is vastly more complex than the computer, can perform many tasks at a time (known as parallel processing) unlike the computers of that era, which utilized the step-by-step technique of serial processing. The computer theory has therefore been left rather high and dry.

ABOVE *The Romantic painter-poet William Blake believed that the "inner eye" is all-important. The figures in his visionary paintings inhabit a dream world, as in this 1795 painting.*

In a similar vein, biophysicist Francis Crick (who co-discovered the double-helix structure of the DNA molecule) and Graeme Mitchison, a mathematician, have suggested that in dreaming sleep the brain is concerned with discarding redundant information that has been taken in during the day. The purpose is to prevent an overload of information, which could cause confusion. It seems a reasonable idea at first sight, but

records of some 350 lucid dreams and presented his observations and ideas. To illustrate the high level of consciousness in the lucid dream, and some of the strange features that characterized it, van Eeden related the following case:

> ❝ I dreamt that I stood at a table before a window. On the table were different objects. I was perfectly well aware that I was dreaming and I considered what sorts of experiments I could make. I began by trying to break glass, by beating it with a stone. Yet it would not break. Then I took a fine claret glass from the table and struck it with my fist, with all my might, at the same time reflecting how dangerous it would be to do this in waking life; yet the glass remained whole. But lo! when I looked at it again after some time, it was broken. It broke all right, but a little too late, like an actor who misses his cue. This gave me a very curious impression of being in a fake world cleverly imitated, but with small failures. ❞

Eye-signalling breakthrough

Sleep laboratory research into lucid dreams was pioneered by Dr. Keith Hearne at Hull University in England. Hearne, after having learned about lucid dreams from the British writer Celia Green's seminal book *Lucid Dreams*, reasoned that it should be possible to communicate to the world of wakefulness in some way. A great problem, though, was that the body is paralysed during dreaming sleep.

However, Dr. Hearne one day remembered that the eye musculature is not inhibited – after all, the state is called rapid-eye-movement sleep (REM). On a hunch, he enlisted the help of a volunteer subject who reported having fairly frequent lucid dreams. The subject was "wired up" in the sleep laboratory (see page 38) and given the instructions that on becoming "lucid" he was immediately to make a sequence of eight extreme left–right eye signals.

On the morning of 12th April 1975 at about 8am, while the subject was in indubitable REM (dreaming) sleep, a series of left–right eye movements was observed in the polygraphic record. On waking, the subject described how, in the dream, he had been walking about in the university when he suddenly became lucid, recalled the instructions to signal, and signalled with his eyes. Dr. Hearne described the experiment as follows:

> ❝ It was like getting the first-ever signals from another solar system. The very chart-record showed that the subject was in a completely different state from wakefulness ('asleep,' 'unconscious,' and 'dreaming') yet he was absolutely conscious and aware of his situation. It was amazing, philosophically. Here was a person in a total reality, which we call a dream, conveying information about what to him was a dream world, which was my waking reality. ❞

Dr. Hearne made the signalling discovery in the sleep laboratory of Hull University and then established a sleep laboratory at Liverpool University. He informed American researchers at Chicago and Stanford of his discovery so that they could make their own investigations. At Liverpool, he completed the world's first Ph.D. research into lucid dreams (submitted May 1978). Dr. Hearne found that although subjects dreamed they were pressing a micro-switch at the same time as making eye signals, because of the general bodily paralysis no signals were produced on that polygraphic trace.

Basic characteristics of lucid dreams

In his extensive research, Dr. Hearne established the basic characteristics of lucid dreams. They were genuine dreams occurring in REM sleep (some had proposed that they are not dreams but a form of vision, or mental imagery, experienced on waking in the night). Their duration is measurable. Signalled information showed that the dreams operated in real time – they were not "over in a flash."

Hearne discovered the "pre-lucid REM burst" – a flurry of eye-movement activity that invariably appears in the chart record before lucidity happens. Its presence indicates that lucidity occurs when cortical stimulation (paralleled by the REM bursts) reaches a critical point.

Also, of course, the signalling technique established, for the first time, a channel of communication from the dream to the waking world. Even telepathy tests were conducted with subjects in the lucid state. Later work by Stephen La Berge, at Stanford University in California, confirmed Dr. Hearne's original findings.

The "light-switch effect"

Dr. Hearne also discovered an important consistent phenomenon in dreams: the "light-switch effect." He asked a group of eight geographically distanced lucid dreamers – who did not know each other, and had no communication between one another – to report back on tasks given to them to perform in the lucid-dream state. None of the subjects could switch on a light in the dream scenery. The dream-producing process manoeuvred the dream so that the light would not suddenly come on – the light-switches had "disappeared," or the bulbs only "glowed dimly," or were "fused."

The effect is interesting because it demonstrates that there are natural, physiologically determined limitations within the dream-producing process. Whatever the current level of "brightness" in a dream, if – using dream control techniques – the dreamer attempts to increase that level rapidly, the system cannot cope and so, it appears, resorts to deceiving the dreamer.

Dr. Hearne warns that there are probably many other such limitations in the dream-constructive system, so we must be cautious about applying meanings to some dream elements which are fundamentally not amenable to interpretation.

ANIMALS' SLEEP

The different animal species exhibit a vast range of sleep experiences. A number of factors influence their patterns, including their size, their metabolic rate, and whether they are predators or prey.

In mammals, the alternation of slow-wave sleep and REM sleep (with animals it is usually termed paradoxical sleep) occurs as in humans – but a curious anomaly has been found to be the Australian spiny ant-eater, which unaccountably seems to show only slow-wave sleep. Grazing animals tend to have little sleep, as do those which sleep in the open or spend a long time feeding. As a general rule, animals that are preyed upon have less paradoxical sleep, while larger animals have more slow-wave sleep. Cats may sleep for up to 16 hours a day. They enter paradoxical sleep roughly every 30 minutes after sleep onset. In that condition, their neck muscles are fully relaxed and slight twitching is sometimes observed. Rabbits do not exhibit muscular paralysis during paradoxical sleep, although their ears are flat though during that period. Horses may sleep only five hours a day – standing 22 hours and having 45 minutes of paradoxical sleep and two hours of slow-wave sleep. Dolphins, strangely, shut down each side of their brain alternately in sleep. They never stop moving and there is no muscular relaxation as in humans and no measurable paradoxical sleep. Probably the arrangement is to permit the dolphin to maintain an awareness and to surface for air occasionally.

Birds also show an alternating cycle between slow-wave sleep and paradoxical sleep. Muscle tone is not lost completely, because they need to roost and maintain posture. Some birds also close down each side of the brain alternately in sleep.

We do not yet know what animals experience during sleep, but anyone who has seen dogs making slight movements and sounds in sleep is bound to assume that the animal is experiencing a vivid dream. And so it may be for many varied species.

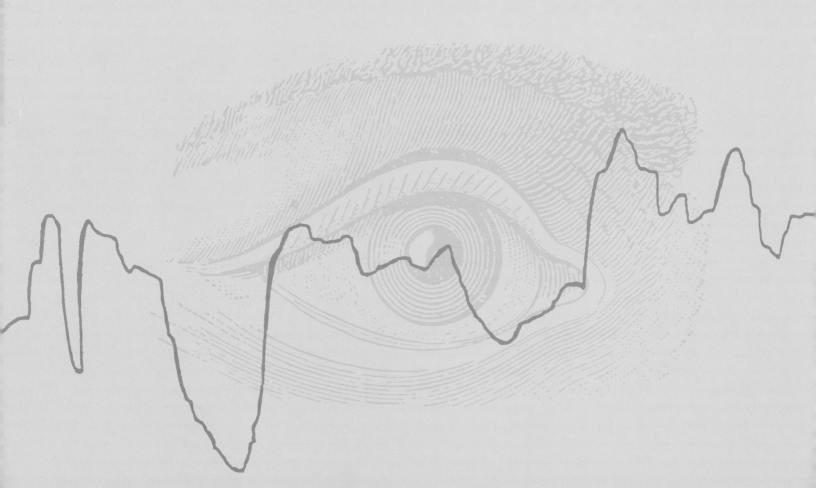

EVERYONE DREAMS, although some people remember their dreams better than other people do. We dream several times a night at regular intervals, for a total of around two hours or so. At the beginning of the night, dreams are very short, but they gradually lengthen as the night progresses, which means that most of our dreaming is done in the second half of the night. As we are nodding off (and occasionally when we are waking up) vivid images sometimes appear, which, like dreams, offer a wealth of potential for enhancing our lives. Some of these images may be premonitions. Indeed, dreams themselves appear to have a strong psychic or paranormal dimension, including not only premonitions but also telepathy.

CYCLES OF SLEEP

As mentioned on page 32, dreaming is accompanied by rapid eye movements, or REM (pronounced to rhyme with "gem"). Even though the eyes are closed, the movements under the eyelids are visible. REM sleep alternates with non-dreaming sleep, with the whole cycle repeating itself every 90 minutes or so. There are usually four or five cycles in a night. The first REM period of the night may last only a minute or so, but with each subsequent cycle it increases in duration, until after about seven or eight hours of sleep the dreaming time can be half an hour or more.

Monitoring sleep and dreaming

Research into sleep and dreaming involves monitoring these cycles in sleep laboratories through the use of electrodes placed on the scalp and body. The subject sleeps in a bedroom and the experimenter monitors the various measures in a separate control room.

The brain's activity is picked up by small, dome-shaped, silver electrodes which are stuck to the scalp. Millionths of a volt may be detected and amplified by powerful circuitry. To ensure that comparisons between studies from different sleep laboratories are valid, an internationally accepted standard system of electrode placements exists.

It is not uncomfortable wearing the electrodes – after a little while, they are not noticed, and the subject can disconnect them easily if necessary. The brainwaves are measured by an electroencephalogram (EEG).

As well as brainwaves, other measures are also recorded, using electrodes stuck to the body, so that several channels of information are presented simultaneously on the chart paper or computer monitor. Eye movements are measured with an electro-oculogram (EOG) and muscle activity with an electromyogram (EMG). Heart rate and breathing

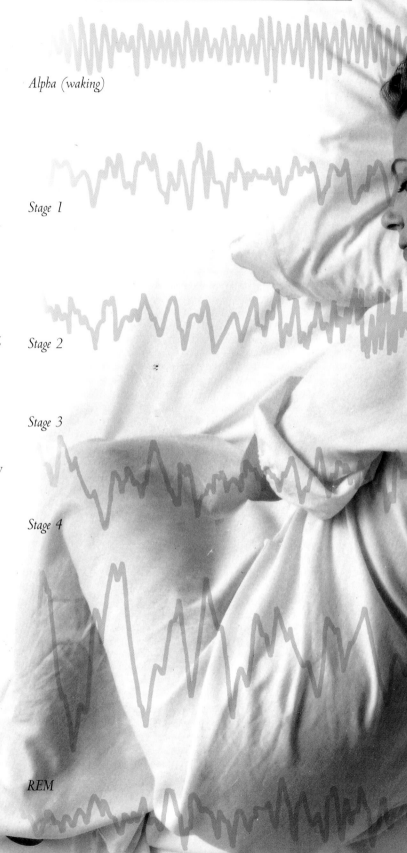

Alpha (waking)

Stage 1

Stage 2

Stage 3

Stage 4

REM

may also be recorded. All of these factors change through the night with the sleep cycles.

The subjects used in sleep-laboratory experiments are often students, or particular groups of people selected to investigate something that could affect sleep and dreams — say, a new drug.

Because the sleep laboratory is a strange environment and the unusual conditions may influence sleep and dreams, the first night of the study is taken to be a settling-in period.

Slow-wave sleep

Non-dreaming sleep has characteristically large, fairly regular, slow waves. It is therefore known as slow-wave sleep (SWS), or sometimes NREM (non-REM) or orthodox sleep. Once a person has fallen asleep, he or she sinks deeper and deeper into SWS. Breathing slows, pulse rate and body temperature drop and the muscles relax.

Slow wave sleep has been sub-divided into four stages, depending on the amount of slow waves present. (Despite the separate categories, the individual stages are not like steps — the transition between them is gradual.) As the stages progress, the waves become slower (lower frequency) and larger (higher voltage).

In Stage I, which occurs when falling asleep, or after body movements during sleep, the brainwaves are of low-voltage, mixed-frequency activity. Many people's eyes roll during this stage, and the amplified movements are very apparent in the chart record. If alpha brainwaves (the waking pattern, about ten cycles per second) are present in the individual, they largely cut out at the start of Stage I. A person disturbed at Stage I would probably deny being asleep — but the physiological changes are already occurring. (Interestingly, when, in an experiment in 1980, Dr. Hearne wired up three people who claimed to be able to achieve "astral-travel" at will, they all entered

Stage I sleep during what they reported as the excursions of their consciousness out of their bodies. For more about "astral travel" and sleep, see page 101.)

Stage 2 sleep exhibits the occasional *K-complex*. This is a fairly large and sudden negative-to-positive wave (see the illustration on pages 38–9) which usually occurs in response to an internal or external stimulus, such as a sudden noise. In the sleep laboratory, a test of this stage is, say, to tap a pen on a surface in the control room. The resulting K-complex from the nearby sleeping subject confirms Stage 2 sleep.

By definition, Stage 3 sleep has 20–50 per cent slow waves of a certain amplitude. As can be seen from the illustration on pages 38–9, the chart record at this point is certainly very different from that of wakefulness.

Stage 4 sleep displays 50 per cent or more slow waves. Whole masses of brain cells are firing in the same pattern, hence the large synchronized waves of two cycles per second or less. It is very deep sleep – breathing is steady and slow and a person woken from this stage shows "sleep drunkenness," being confused and disoriented. This is restorative sleep, when the outflow of tissue-building hormones increases and cell regeneration occurs.

REM sleep

It is always fascinating to watch the chart record change to that of REM sleep. The large waves subside over several minutes and the different measures alter drastically. The brainwaves lessen in magnitude and increase in frequency, as a busy, "sawtooth" wave-form appears, more like the patterns of someone who is awake (see the illustration on pages 38–9).

The eye-movement channels, which were in effect simply picking up the high-voltage brain activity, now show relatively straight traces, but with occasional bursts of activity – rapid eye movements – lasting several seconds. The two electrodes positioned below the jawline to pick up "sub-mental" muscle

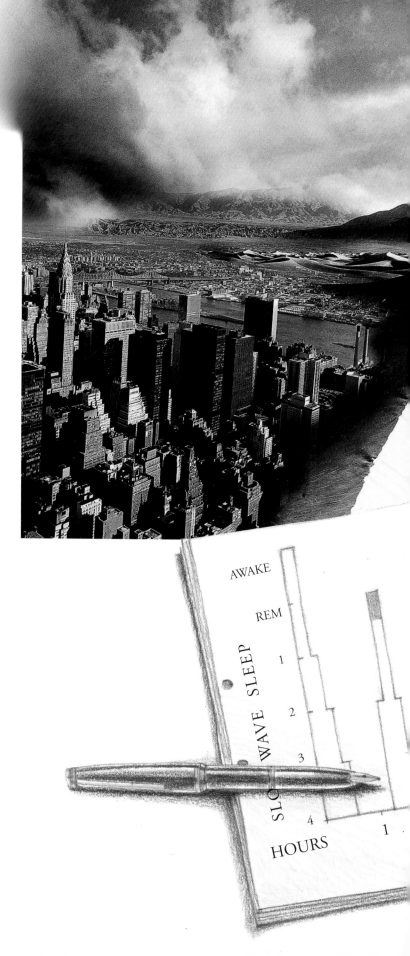

TYPICAL SLEEP PATTERN

movements now record very little activity. Breathing is shallow, irregular and rapid, and the pulse and blood pressure are higher.

One intriguing aspect of REM sleep is that males develop a penile erection and females a clitoral erection. However, as mentioned on page 30, this arousal cycle appears to be physiologically based. The erection is not there because of the dream content (although dreams can modify the degree of arousal, so that a fearful dream, say, can lead to detumescence).

Breathing is an automatic process, but the rest of the musculature (except the eye muscles) is inhibited. The muscles are relaxed and flaccid, and signals from the brain to the muscles are blocked, so that the subject is, in effect, paralysed. The paralysis is profound: humans merely twitch slightly in REM sleep. This is the state associated with dreaming – which is presumably so that we are unable to act out our dreams. Nature protects us.

Significance of the two types of sleep

When the progress of the various sleep states and stages is plotted graphically, the diagram known as "sleep architecture" results (see the illustration on the left). This illustrates how the amount and depth of SWS decreases during the course of the night, while the amount of REM sleep increases each time it makes an appearance. Thus, in broad terms, the first half of the night consists mostly of SWS, while the second half is mostly REM sleep.

People deprived of sleep spend more time in the slow-wave state once they can sleep again. REM sleep, strangely, does not seem to be too significant. Short-term deprivation of REM sleep does lead to a "rebound effect," so that when the cause of the REM deprivation is removed, a higher proportion of sleep will initially be REM. This is a physiological phenomenon; but if REM sleep is abolished over several months – say, by certain drugs – there are no noticeable harmful effects.

So what is the purpose of REM sleep? It may be that in adults it is left over from an earlier function. Newborn babies exhibit REM sleep about half the time they are slumbering. Perhaps it is especially important in the foetus for stimulating the brain, setting up circuitry – or even providing entertainment.

Similarly, although we know that the stages of the sleep cycle are the result of chemical changes in sequence at sites at the base of the brain, we do not know the purpose of the cycles – or even of sleep itself. We do know, however, that dreams contain information that can be useful to the dreamer.

THE NATURE OF DREAMS

From all the accumulated evidence available, it seems that a dream is a sequence of moving images, based on a significant thought which may be either conscious or unconscious. The imagery progresses along associative pathways (sequences in which one image influences the next) in the brain. These are verbal – involving puns, for example – or visual. The associations by which the dream progresses are personal to the dreamer.

In dreaming sleep, sensory thresholds are high, which means that many sensations and sounds will not be noticed. Yet it is certainly the case that external stimuli can be incorporated into an ongoing dream. For example, cold may be directly incorporated so that the dreamer dreams of, say, being in snow or ice. Or the stimulus may be indirectly assimilated so that, perhaps, the ring of an alarm clock may be transformed within the dream into someone shouting. A "dream machine" invented by Dr. Hearne used electric pulses to the wrist as a consistent form of external stimulation to induce lucidity.

At one time there was a question as to whether we dream in colour. In 1962 American researcher Edwin Kahn and his team found that when subjects were woken from REM sleep in a sleep laboratory, some 70 per cent of the reports referred to colours in the interrupted dream – either spontaneously or if specifically asked. It seems that colour, although present, is soon forgotten in preference to remembering the activities within the dream.

One of the very noticeable characteristics of dreams is that they fade rapidly from memory. Although we dream for about two hours a night, we only recall a dream if we awaken immediately after (or during) it, and we tend only to remember fragments the next day. Yet something that happens the following day can sometimes bring a whole dream flooding back. It is as if the dream had been filed away somewhere else rather than erased. One compelling reason for the rapid suppression of most dream material could be that it might otherwise become confused with real events and memories.

Studies have shown that the amount of dreaming sleep that people experience declines somewhat with age. In a major study in Florida in 1974, Robert Williams, Karacan and Carolyn Hursch found that the average amount of REM sleep per night for toddlers was 186 minutes (31 per cent of their sleeping time), for 20–29 year-olds 116 minutes (27 per cent) and for 70–79 year-olds 92 minutes (23 per cent). The amount of deep (Stage 3 and 4) sleep also correspondingly declined, to 120, 86 and 23 minutes respectively. Light (Stage 1 and 2) sleep constituted the remaining part.

BORDERLAND PHENOMENA

During Stage 1, which is the nodding-off stage between consciousness and sleep, very vivid images – as opposed to dreams – can appear. This *hypnagogic imagery*, as it is known, can vary considerably, from startling warnings and vivid premonitions to static scenes or even voices.

The most common hypnagogic imagery is of a simple nature. Many people report seeing an eye gazing at them, while others witness apparitions of familiar and unfamiliar faces. Some see people walking towards them, and others observe nonsensical "action" scenes. Sometimes entire conversations are heard, occasionally in a foreign tongue.

In sleep research generally, the importance of the hypnagogic state is perhaps underestimated. Researchers tend to accept that it represents the onset of sleep but are more interested in other sleep phenomena. This underlines the point that, as far as knowledge about sleep and dreams is concerned, we are merely scratching the surface. Within the realm of hypnagogic imagery lies a mysterious world which, if better understood, could offer considerable rewards.

Warnings

One type of hypnagogic imagery is the warning. Warnings are commonly reported in times of stress or danger. For example, late one night shortly after the end of the Second World War, Brian L., an exhausted British soldier on guard duty in Germany, was nodding off. He was startled awake by the voice of his father, who screamed, "Brian, watch out!" He regained awareness just in time to avoid being attacked from behind by a resentful German ex-soldier. At the time, Brian's father was fast asleep back in England.

Perhaps less common, but just as important, are cases that occur when the dreamer is not exposed to danger in such an obvious way. During 1981, after the death of her husband Bill, Joan N. had been experiencing difficulty in getting to sleep. This particular night, she decided to try to relax with a cigarette and a hot cup of tea.

> 66 *I must have nodded off. The next thing I knew was Bill shouting, 'Joan, wake up!' I opened my eyes to discover my cigarette hovering precariously over the settee, and the hot tea was just about to spill. Clearly, if I hadn't woken when I did, at the very least I might have been scalded, but I could have just as easily set fire to myself. There is no doubt in my mind whatsoever that it was my husband who had called out. Since then, I have always known that he is still with me.* 99

Soon after retiring for the night, Fleur C., a young lady who was camping in northern India, snuggled up in her sleeping bag. As she was dozing, she heard her name called loud enough to wake her. When she opened her eyes, she discovered that something flammable had been spilt on the floor and had ignited around her. This warning enabled her to make her escape.

Often people can recall that while falling asleep they heard their names being called. In fact, this is so common that many readers of this book will be familiar with the experience. However, when they sit up and turn on the light, nobody is present and there is no apparent danger. Some people might hear a loud bang, or even sense that they have been struck on the head — bright flashes of light might also be seen.

Also typical of this early stage of sleep is the muscle spasm known as the *myoclonic jerk*, due to natural changes in the nervous system. The sudden shock affects any imagery that is occurring, so that the individual reacts accordingly — they hear a gunshot, say, or think that they have stumbled. A sensation of falling may feature, too.

Sleep-onset premonitions

Precognitive visions (premonitions) seen during hypnagogic imagery are said to be particularly reliable and rarely need interpreting because they usually reflect future events fairly accurately.

Both authors are familiar with the extraordinary precognitive abilities of Barbara Garwell, a sweet, gentle lady who is a housewife. Dr. Hearne has for

years made a special study of Barbara's premonitions, and as we shall see later in this book, several of her "future viewings" have emerged in the hypnagogic state. In one year-long study, Barbara was asked to send all her premonitions to Dr. Hearne, so that he could witness and document the visions before the events occurred (normally 21 days after her premonition – see page 54).

However, on Monday, 10th May 1982, Barbara experienced a premonition concerning Pope John Paul II, which made such a powerful impression on her that she telephoned Dr. Hearne personally, then sent a written account.

> **"** *As I got into bed I closed my eyes and saw the outside of a castle. From the castle came about eight choir-boys or altar-boys. There were a lot of people together and much confusion. In the centre of these people I saw a figure in white. It was a person of state; e.g. the Pope.* **"**

Just three days later, at the Fatima shrine in Portugal, an attempt was made on the Pope's life – a man tried to bayonet him. Although Barbara had failed to see the assassination attempt in her vision, she knew instinctively that something significant was going to happen concerning the Pope. In reality, there was indeed much confusion around the man in white!

Another of Barbara's hypnagogic visions occurred at the end of March 1982:

> **"** *I got into bed and shut my eyes. I got a clear picture, as if on a cinema screen. It was an island with whitish buildings. It seemed to move as if projected to me (the length of the island). It was not a big island. There was a huge stretch of what seemed to be bluish water in front of it. Then I saw lots and lots of boats. It seemed to me that they were facing each other for attack. They were definitely boats, not ships. Across the front of this screen was a whole length of*

foreign words that I could not understand. It was so real; like watching a TV screen. This was the clearest visual experience I have ever had. **"**

Exactly three days later, on 2nd April 1982, the Falkland/Malvinas Islands were invaded by Argentine military forces. During the televised coverage of the conflict, British broadcasters often showed scenes with Spanish text on the screen – as Barbara had seen it.

Problem-solving

During the transition between consciousness and sleep, the first link to the curious workings of the subconscious is established – a kind of hypnagogic bridge. It makes sense, therefore, if the *oneironaut* (dream traveller) can find ways to utilize this curious state – perhaps to access warnings, premonitions and insights into the dreamer's own life.

David Melbourne, who experiences a high degree of visual imagery, utilizes this condition for various purposes, which include his pioneering technique

for problem-solving. Over the years, Melbourne has trained himself to remain in the hypnagogic state for hours if he wishes, without succumbing to the next stage of sleep. He has become adept at conjuring up people, animating them and observing the outcome of their actions. One day he had the idea of presenting them with a problem similar to a situation in his life, then scrutinizing how these invented characters dealt with the issues that arose.

One particular issue that had been troubling him concerned a friend he met occasionally at social gatherings. Generally, he got on very well with this individual and they had much in common. However, there were occasions when the person, for no apparent reason, seemed to go out of his way to avoid conversation. As the friend was usually a reliable, steady man, these incidents often led Melbourne to wonder if he had done or said something out of place.

Entering hypnagogic imagery, he decided to conjure up this individual along with a likeness of himself, animate them, observe the scene as it developed, and see if he could find a clue as to why this person seemed to blow hot and cold.

Immediately, Melbourne observed that his invented characters were standing on grass. Then, to his surprise, he witnessed a snake slither up to this

individual and, as it spat at Melbourne, using its tail as a lever, it pushed the friend away from him.

Melbourne was alerted to the possibility of the involvement of a third party who didn't feel comfortable with him. This led him to pay close attention to the company in which he found himself on occasions when his friend appeared to be indifferent. Indeed, it transpired that a third party, who appeared to be covetous of Melbourne's friend, seemed annoyed when Melbourne was around. Perhaps his friend had sensed this and, in order to placate the third party, was keeping Melbourne at arm's length.

Alerted to this possibility, he made an effort to involve the other person more in conversation and get

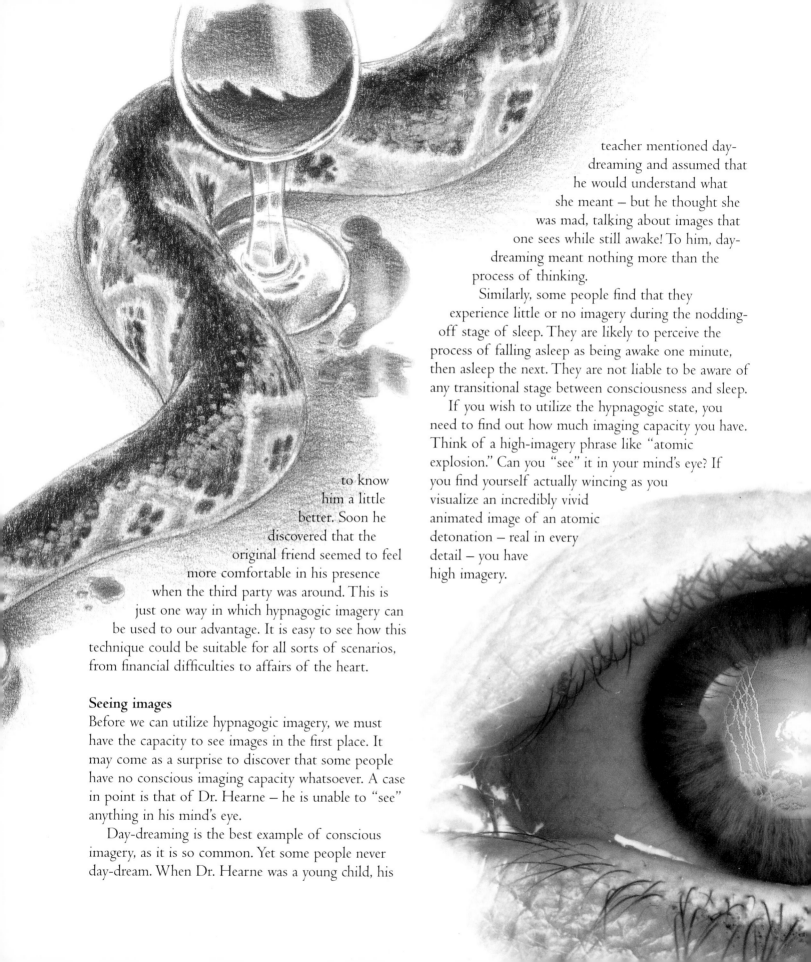

teacher mentioned day-dreaming and assumed that he would understand what she meant – but he thought she was mad, talking about images that one sees while still awake! To him, day-dreaming meant nothing more than the process of thinking.

Similarly, some people find that they experience little or no imagery during the nodding-off stage of sleep. They are likely to perceive the process of falling asleep as being awake one minute, then asleep the next. They are not liable to be aware of any transitional stage between consciousness and sleep.

If you wish to utilize the hypnagogic state, you need to find out how much imaging capacity you have. Think of a high-imagery phrase like "atomic explosion." Can you "see" it in your mind's eye? If you find yourself actually wincing as you visualize an incredibly vivid animated image of an atomic detonation – real in every detail – you have high imagery.

to know him a little better. Soon he discovered that the original friend seemed to feel more comfortable in his presence when the third party was around. This is just one way in which hypnagogic imagery can be used to our advantage. It is easy to see how this technique could be suitable for all sorts of scenarios, from financial difficulties to affairs of the heart.

Seeing images

Before we can utilize hypnagogic imagery, we must have the capacity to see images in the first place. It may come as a surprise to discover that some people have no conscious imaging capacity whatsoever. A case in point is that of Dr. Hearne – he is unable to "see" anything in his mind's eye.

Day-dreaming is the best example of conscious imagery, as it is so common. Yet some people never day-dream. When Dr. Hearne was a young child, his

If you are able to imagine the explosion, but not in such sharp detail, you have good imagery. If you have to struggle to bring the scene to your mind's eye, you have only slight imagery. And if you see nothing at all, you have no imagery.

In the latter case, there is still a way you can join the ranks of accomplished imagers and put the hypnagogic state to good use. Whether you are aware of this transitional stage of nodding off or not, at some point after retiring you will become "dozy": that is when you are in the hypnagogic state.

This state provides a good opportunity for self-hypnosis (see page 79), or for reinforcing positive thought patterns. It is the best time to resolve to give up smoking, stop nail-biting, or lose those extra pounds. We often hear about long-term smokers who suddenly announce they have given up the habit. "One day, I just woke up and decided to stop," seems to be a common theme – but perhaps this decision has not been arrived at by chance!

Persisting imagery on waking

Many people report that they have occasionally had visions, or mental images, that lingered for a time – generally a few seconds – after waking up. This type of persisting vision is termed *hypnopompic imagery*.

Usually, of course, the opposite happens: the moment you open your eyes, your dreams just melt away. If you are interested in dream analysis, this can be annoying, as you will desperately be trying to cling on to tantalizing memories, which seem to hover just out of reach.

Consequently, if you do experience hypnopompic imagery, you have an advantage. You will be able to capitalize on these lingering visions by memorizing and consolidating the dream's content, so that it can be easily recorded. Even this seemingly benign dream condition can be put to a constructive use.

SLEEP PARALYSIS

Perhaps the most startling of all dream states is that of sleep paralysis. It occurs on the very edge of consciousness, but in this case the dreamer is still in REM sleep and therefore totally paralysed. Some people are not at all bothered by sleep paralysis, and can even regard it as an interesting episode. Often, however, these experiences can be extremely frightening.

Sleep paralysis has been known as "night-nurses' paralysis" because the condition is found more often in people who work a night-shift, and who are liable to fall asleep when vigilance is required. The unconscious knows that sleep is inappropriate at that time, so an expectation of being discovered results in a dream of someone approaching.

With sleep paralysis, it appears that cortical arousal occurs, so that the person becomes conscious, but physically the individual is still in REM sleep and therefore constrained. Invariably, they are absolutely convinced that they are wide awake. They have full long-term and short-term memory and identity, and everything in the bedroom or workplace in the dream is a vivid, exact replica of the real surroundings. Some people imagine that they are dying, having a stroke, in a cataleptic trance, or the victim of some malevolent force. In reality, these are REM sleep experiences.

Often the individual thinks they are making loud sounds when in fact they are not, because of the paralysis. Such was the case with June J., who described her experience as follows:

> **66** *I thought I'd died. I tried to signal to my husband to wake me up. I tried to nudge him but I couldn't move. All I wanted to do was to wake up. I tried to make a noise. I thought I did, but he said he didn't hear anything. It really worried me.* **99**

In another case, a woman telephoned for a doctor because her mother was making odd gurgling noises while asleep. In fact, the mother was experiencing sleep paralysis and the noise was the slight result of her frantic efforts to

communicate. The doctor was, surprisingly, uninformed about the condition of sleep paralysis.

Buried alive!
Robert D. reported the following childhood experiences:

> **66** *As a child I often woke up terrified. I thought I was biting and shouting at my mother. When I really woke up she hadn't felt or heard anything. I still experience this thing. I've tried to relax and pray. I'm afraid someone will think I'm dead and I'll be buried alive.* **99**

These experiences are frightening enough, but the following examples become progressively more fearful. The first report is from Loraine V.:

> **66** *I imagined that somebody was lying in bed with me, but I couldn't see who it was because I was struggling to turn over but couldn't move.* **99**

Celia C. repeats this theme – in chilling detail. Her husband Jim works as a chauffeur, and Celia only experiences sleep paralysis if he leaves for work in the early hours.

> **66** *My husband always bends down to kiss me and says, 'Good-bye.' I reply, 'Good-bye, take care.' After a short while, he returns and bends down to kiss me again. I say, 'I thought you had left already.' Then, I notice that this person has no face. I try to push it away but cannot move.*
>
> *On another occasion, I kissed my husband good-bye, then thought that he was still in bed. I saw somebody beside me, and told him that I thought he had gone to work. This body rolled out from beneath the sheets and under the bed.* **99**

Not all such experiences are as disconcerting. Occasionally, they can be accompanied by a feeling of comfort, as in Rosalie M.'s account:

I heard someone coming up the stairs. I thought it was a relative who had been doing a job for me. I remember thinking that it couldn't be, because it was far too early. I tried to open my eyes but couldn't. Then I tried calling out but no sound left my lips. I heard the door open. Then I felt a hand on my forehead. It was comforting. Still my eyes were shut tightly. Then, slowly, I woke up, expecting to see somebody, but the room was empty. I wasn't frightened. Nothing was said and nobody was seen.

Alien abductions

In psychology, expectation is acknowledged to have a powerful effect. For instance, if people expect to go into a trance at a spiritual healing venue and writhe around on the floor, the moment hands have been laid on them, it is likely that this will happen. Likewise, it has been known since ancient times that dreams can be incubated through expectation (see pages 14 and 15). Many people are even able to induce the dreams of their desire, by consciously willing them, with a degree of excited anticipation. Cases of sleep paralysis are similar, because there is conscious awareness — and when there is conscious awareness, what you think is what you will dream.

This fact has a bearing on today's interest in "alien abductions" (in which beings from another world supposedly abduct a person temporarily, perhaps for the purposes of experimentation). Nowadays, there are more and more reports on the subject; in fact, it is difficult to turn a page of a newspaper or magazine, or tune in to radio or television broadcasts, without being bombarded with such reports. The world of TV fiction is cashing in, too, with programmes like *The X Files* and *Dark Skies*.

It seems hardly surprising, then, that reports of alien abductions in the bedroom are on the increase. One feature which remains constant in these accounts is that abductees always state that, during these experiences, they find they are paralysed.

In reality, if they have recently read or heard an account of an alien abduction and then they experience a period of sleep paralysis for the first time, it is feasible that they might link it to an abduction incident. This is where the effect of expectation can take over. The moment that thought flits through the mind, they are likely to dream it.

In extreme instances of sleep paralysis, people have been so traumatized that they have been left with physical manifestations of the experience. In 1996, a case resulted in a woman's hair turning white overnight. Emma D. described her terrifying experience as follows:

> 66 *I woke up totally unable to move. Then, to my horror, I found a creature, which I imagined was the devil, licking my neck!* 99

There is obviously every reason to learn how to control this sometimes frightening episode. The technique is to "label" the condition as soon as you recognize your inability to move. Then relax. Don't fight it. Ignore any dream imagery. You will immediately sink back into sleep and come out of the sleep paralysis naturally when the REM period ends. (For more about this type of technique, see page 81.)

DREAMS AND THE PARANORMAL

It would be grossly unscientific, unreasonable and censorious not to include here information about dreams that appear to have a paranormal aspect. Orthodox science has more or less dictated that such "psychic" phenomena are not permitted to exist, but the plain fact is and always has been that there are too many cases to ignore. Anomalies in any area of research indicate that the current thinking is erroneous in some way. To pretend not to know of relevant data is a cardinal crime in science – which should seek to find the truth, even if all the comfortable earlier concepts have to be irrevocably overthrown.

Telepathic dreams
Telepathic dreams occur when the dreamer seems to pick up information about an event somewhere while it is happening – it is as if the dreamer were reading the mind of someone present. Considerable research was carried out in this field in England over a century ago, in 1886, by Gurney, Myers and Podmore, some of the founders of the Society for Psychical Research, and reported in *Phantasms of the Living*. It was found

that, often, the dream would provide unexpected information about a person – say, that they were ill or in an unusual predicament. There were many reports of people dreaming of the death of someone at the precise time it happened.

Dream telepathy has been studied in the sleep laboratory. In a series of well-designed experiments at the Maimonides Hospital in New York in the 1960s, Montague Ullman and Stanley Krippner found evidence of a telepathic effect happening in the dream state.

In the experiments a "receiver" was wired up and woken after each REM period to give an account of any dreams. Each time the receiver was dreaming, the awake "sender" tried to influence the dreams of the subject by concentrating on

certain material that had been selected randomly. Different target material was selected over the several nights of the experiment. "Blind" judges (who were ignorant of what had been "sent") later rated the amount of association. Statistical tests determined the likelihood of telepathy being responsible.

In one study, the sender focused on a specific painting each night. The target pictures and results were: 1 *Bedtime* by Keene (Miss), 2 *Yellow Rabbi* by Chagall (Hit), 3 *The Sacrament of the Last Supper* by Dali (Hit), 4 *School of the Dance* by Degas (Hit), 5 *Paris Through a Window* by Chagall (Hit), 6 *Persistence of Memory* by Dali (Hit), 7 *Apples and Oranges* by Cézanne (Miss).

Precognitive dreams

About 40 per cent of reported psychic experiences concern knowing the future in some way, and dreams are the most common form in which precognitions (premonitions) appear. These dreams appear to anticipate a later unexpected event, which could not reasonably have been inferred from information available at the time of the dream. Premonitions also occur (in descending order of importance) in the form of waking thoughts, waking imagery and hypnagogic imagery (see page 44).

Throughout all recorded human history, there have been reports of precognitive dreams, a number of which are described on pages 16, 21–2 and 26.

Dr. Hearne conducted extensive research into premonitions after he experienced apparent foreknowledge of an accident while travelling on a ferry. He found that people who experience these precognitive dreams are mainly female, and the premonitions mostly concern untoward events that will happen to people close to the *percipient* (the person having the premonition).

He categorized different types of premonition and discovered an interesting sub-group which he labelled the "media announcement type." This is where the dreamer receives a very realistic communication in the dream – say, from a radio, TV or newspaper announcement about an event that has not yet happened. This variety seems to be particularly accurate. They may be fairly frequent and nevertheless often go unnoticed, as the time discrepancy is not usually appreciated.

Dr. Hearne found, with some of his subjects, a consistent *latency period*, or delay, between the premonition and the later event. Barbara Garwell (see page 44), for instance, often displayed such an effect: in her case it was 21 days. Thus, in September 1981, Barbara dreamed of a group of dignitaries at a stadium in a Middle Eastern country. A number of soldiers ran up to the rows of men and sprayed them with automatic gunfire. Twenty-one days later, on 6th October 1981, President Anwar Sadat of Egypt was assassinated and several other people killed or injured at an identical event, commemorating the 1973 Yom Kippur war with Israel.

The big philosophical problem about premonitions is, of course, the fact that the effect (knowledge of the event) appears to precede the cause (the event). This is a theoretical impossibility to *current* conventional science – just as it was once thought "impossible" that the sun did not go around the earth.

Some of the counter-theories that have been put forward to explain premonitions are that the events could be inferred, that they are just coincidences or that only good cases are used. Other, more extreme explanations have included telepathy, clairvoyance, and particles travelling faster than the speed of light (and so technically arriving before they left).

Parapsychological experiments in guessing which card will be shown next, or which light on a panel will illuminate next, have provided considerable statistical evidence for foreknowledge. Because of the staggering and consistent amount of evidence supporting the existence of premonitions, "official science" in the new millennium will have to change – drastically – in order to accommodate observations that it has long suppressed or repressed.

Shared dreams

Sometimes people discover – usually accidentally – that they have experienced a virtually identical dream, perhaps at the same time. In this variety of shared dream, two or more people seem to experience the same events and have similar images. As an example, two people might both report having dreamt of mending the same component on a car.

A variation of this type is where two or more people have the same dream, but separated by a period of time. Yvonne H. was married to an airline pilot and experienced a recurring dream which stopped troubling her around the time of her husband's death. She dreamed of getting into an elevator, and pressing the button to go down to the basement. However, the elevator accelerated upwards, gathering tremendous speed until it burst through the roof, at which point Yvonne would wake up. She never told anybody about these dreams. Five years later, she was staying with her daughter in Dubai. While out for a drive together, Yvonne's daughter described a peculiar dream she had recently experienced: it was identical to Yvonne's dream.

In another kind of shared dream, one person seems to be present in another's dream, or in more than one person's dream, and observes what is happening. Thus, Sheila R. reports:

> 66 *I had a dream of something, a creature of some kind, on my back. I awoke with an unpleasant feeling. A few seconds later my young daughter ran into my bedroom saying, 'Mummy, are you all right? I dreamed that something was on your back!'* 99

Shared dreams may be much more common than we imagine, because the discussion of dreams is usually fairly limited. The theoretical implications are fascinating. Are they caused by the dreams using a common symbol representing a similar thought concerning something that happened in the day? Or is a type of telepathy happening between the dreamers? Can a part of your consciousness actually enter someone else's mind? These questions need to be explored. Such anomalies often act as clues that lead to great new discoveries.

Dreams heralding illness

Some dreams appear to give a symbolic or even a direct indication of something, in particular an illness, that has not yet appeared physically in the dreamer. These are known as *prodromic dreams* (prodromic means "before running"). Thus, a worrying, perplexing dream or series of dreams about a system of underground pipes could refer to an impending vascular condition.

The usual rationale for prodromic dreams is that the unconscious has such an intimate link to the body that it becomes aware of minuscule symptoms long before they can be consciously perceived. The dream provides the communication channel to consciousness – though, of course, the information may not be interpreted and appreciated.

In fact, two additional possibilities exist here. One is that the unconscious might actually cause the physical condition. The other theoretical possibility is that the advance information arrives, via some psychic means, as a premonition – before anything can possibly be either detected or caused. We must not allow any biases of thinking to influence us here; we must look only at the facts. Here is an example of an apparent symbolic indicator of developing illness, as reported by John R.:

I had an upsetting dream in which I was holding a baby and running along a clifftop, being pursued by my brother-in-law – who was shouting to me to drop the baby. Suddenly a man in a black cloak appeared in front of me. The man held up a large crucifix and told me to hand over the baby. However, on looking at the child, I saw that it had turned into an ugly creature. As I looked at it, the creature gave out a terrible howl, lashing its long tongue round the top of my arm and I felt this painful burn and dropped the baby. The pain was still present that morning as I was telling my wife about the dream. A few days later a rash developed at the site and shingles was diagnosed. Interestingly, I discovered later that shingles was in earlier times known as the curse of Satan.

The same man told of a second dream that he'd had, which was also a symbolic indicator of developing illness:

I dreamed that I was sleeping on a water bed but that it developed a leak. I had a finger in the hole trying to stop the water escaping. I woke up with my finger pressed into my navel. I was taken into hospital a few days later with a cyst near my navel.

A dream diagnosis that Suzie S. had may have saved her life:

I was living in California. I worked in a hospital. I'd recently had my annual physical examination, including a cervical smear. I dreamed that a man, maybe eight feet tall, dressed in white, stood before me. He told me I had cancer. I decided to go anonymously for an extra examination at a woman's clinic. Three days later I received a call telling me that I had a positive result indicating a pre-cancerous condition. I had surgery.

A dream cure seems to have been given to Rebecca H.:

> " *I was in hospital expecting a baby. My blood pressure was extremely high and no medications could lower it. One night, after two weeks of being in hospital, I dreamt that my granddad, who is dead, walked into the ward and handed me a tiny bottle with some dark substance inside. He told me to drink it — so I did. After the dream that night, the night nurse took my blood pressure. It was still high. However, in the morning I was told that my blood pressure had gone back to normal. The doctor looking at my chart said that it was a miracle. I wanted to tell them what had happened that night, but I thought they would laugh at me.* "

Some cases seem to include a psychic, precognitive component, as in Debbie P.'s dream:

> " *In my dream, I was looking down on myself in an operating theatre and could see a man leaning over me. He turned around and I could see he was a surgeon cutting open my throat. The dream ended there and although it was disturbing, I quickly put it out of my mind. Two years later I started to have problems with my eyes and needed an operation for an over-active thyroid in my throat. When I met the surgeon I was amazed to find he looked just like the man who operated on me in my dream!* "

The power of the unconscious

To assume that the dream simply reflects unconsciously detected symptoms is to put the unconscious in an uncharacteristically passive role. We know that the unconscious is capable of improving a person's state of health — for example, a positive attitude in a person stricken with illness can sometimes cause a miraculous reversal in what might usually be a downward path.

By the same token, the unconscious can also cause a range of illnesses or even death. The so-called "conversion reaction neurosis" is an example of the power of the unconscious over the body. In this condition, a person with a neurotic frame of mind who is refusing to acknowledge a particular problem in their life develops a metaphorical physical symptom, such as hysterical blindness. Another example is the power of the curse, one of the oldest forms of magic; the Aboriginal "bone-pointing" curse, for

instance, can apparently sometimes cause the death of the selected victim.

We must accept that some prodromic dreams probably reflect an intention on the part of the unconscious to hurt the individual. The reason is not sensible and does not aid self-protection, so it must be for some distorted, psychological purpose concerning an unresolved issue. Darwinian self-preservation does not enter into the equation in such cases.

It is rather mind-blowing to consider that some of our illnesses may be self-inflicted symbols of an inner psychological conflict.

Foreseeing one's future health

It is even more of a challenge to conventional logic to think that the future state of one's body can be viewed in dreams – yet that may actually be the case. When the impossible has been entirely eliminated, then whatever remains, no matter how unlikely, must be the truth. We must therefore adjust our mind-sets accordingly and not pretend otherwise.

If the unconscious does function as a passive illness-detector, dreamers might utilize "lucid" dreams – in which they become conscious and can manipulate the dream – to conjure up a "dream doctor" who, using fantastic equipment, can diagnose future illnesses (see page 94 for more about this). Or, if the alternative theories accounting for prodromic dreams are correct, the unconscious could be detecting illnesses that the individual is going to make happen, or it may perhaps be allowing the individual's medical future to be observed by supernormal means. Whatever the process, this is a potentially very important area for medical research because it could give incredibly useful forewarning of bodily malfunction.

SLEEP DISORDERS & NIGHTMARES

Most people experience a sleep problem at some time in their lives, but many will quickly respond to treatment. Insomnia is one of the most common yet is none the less distressing. Many sleep disorders are associated with slow-wave (deep, non-dreaming) sleep, including sleepwalking, sleep-talking, teeth-grinding, bedwetting and snoring. A small percentage of nightmares also occur during slow-wave sleep, but the vast majority of nightmares take place during dreaming sleep. One of the most effective therapies for a wide range of

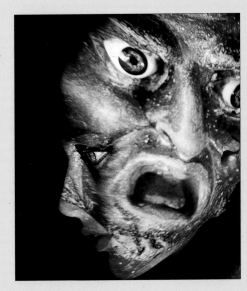

sleep problems, from insomnia to nightmares, involves utilizing the power of suggestion, and this chapter includes several "scripts" to enable sufferers to tackle these sleeping problems themselves.

INSOMNIA

About one in three people report that they have had difficulty in sleeping at some time. Because humans differ so much, though, some people who have disturbed sleep, or little sleep, do not classify themselves as insomniacs whereas some individuals who have, in fact, a fairly substantial amount of sleep do put themselves in this category! Insomnia therefore is the subjective *complaint* of insufficient sleep.

The theories behind insomnia are certainly varied. A psychoanalyst, for example, might be of the opinion that the condition is to do with repressed fears or wishes. Perhaps the individual associates sleep with death, or maybe there is a realization of the crude wishes that lurk in one's dreams, either of which could result in an avoidance of sleeping.

Insomnia is a fairly specialized subject and can have many causes. However, probably the most common is that of stress, and it is this area on which we shall concentrate.

The amount of sleep required varies from person to person. One individual might cope well on four hours a night, while another finds it difficult to manage with less than nine or ten hours – or even more. On average, about eight hours can be considered a sufficient amount for most people to function efficiently throughout the day.

Curiously, it has been established that there are some who wildly overestimate the extent of the insomnia from which they suffer. Many partners are surprised when a spouse complains of a sleepless night as, each time they themselves have awakened during the night, they have been greeted with the sound of gentle snoring. This suggests that some

people actually dream of insomnia, and may even be experiencing several false awakenings (see page 97).

Types of insomnia

Broadly speaking, stress-related insomnia falls into two categories: "initial insomnia," when a person has a problem falling asleep on going to bed, and "sleep-maintenance insomnia," which means awakening during the night and then having difficulty going back to sleep.

In initial insomnia, a person feels unable to shut down mentally – they tend to keep going over the day's complications or other preoccupations. Sleep-maintenance insomniacs may, upon waking, find themselves planning the day ahead, or even beginning to worry about an ongoing problem. In both instances, stress is a common cause.

Various personality studies have been made on insomniacs. Although the results are inconsistent regarding sleep-maintenance insomniacs, the studies show that initial insomniacs tend to be a little neurotic and suffer from depression and anxiety.

Both types of insomnia can become habits. Under these circumstances, worrying about the insomnia is likely to make matters worse, as a vicious circle results. The less sleep, the more worry, which leads to less sleep. In these instances, it is important to recognize the effect of this negative thinking and to change your mind-set from one of "I know I'm going to have another sleepless night," to "Half my trouble has been due to my concern about insomnia. Tonight, I'm not going to give it a second thought."

However, that is just one small weapon in the armory against stress-related insomnia. There are many more simple measures that can be taken to alleviate the problem.

A suitable environment

It is surprising how many people do not pay enough attention to the environment in which they are going to spend a third of their lives – namely the bedroom. For example, it is not unheard of for someone automatically to select the master bedroom in which to sleep, when a busy main road is just the other side of the window. All that might be needed to deal with their insomnia is to choose a smaller room at the back of the house, where it is quiet.

Another way of dealing with background noise is the subtle use of neutral "white noise," such as a gentle water fountain, a ticking clock or an electric fan, for example. Earplugs can be effective for light sleepers who wake at the slightest thing.

There are other factors to consider, too. Make sure that the colour scheme is pleasant and conducive to relaxation: soft pastels are particularly appropriate. Be fussy about the lighting in the room – again, soft lighting is preferable to a glaring bulb. Determining the ideal temperature for your well-being is important, too. And, of course, a well-supporting, comfortable bed is a must.

Developing a routine

Regular habits play an important part in obtaining a good night's sleep – the system becomes used to it. An initial insomniac is likely to benefit from a regular programme of "winding down" as bedtime approaches. A sleep-maintenance insomniac, however, is likely to enjoy a more satisfying sleep if they increase the amount of physical and mental exercise they take during the day. As far as possible try to retire at the same time every night.

Watch what you eat and drink at bedtime. Some people can't sleep on an empty stomach, while others have difficulty sleeping if they have just eaten. Individuals will be aware of which food and liquids tend to keep their stomach churning – everyone is different. Hot malted-milk drinks are sometimes helpful for initial insomniacs, while caffeine (yes, caffeine) may benefit some sleep-maintenance insomniacs, who are thought to be under-stimulated.

Sleeping tablets are not recommended as the answer to insomnia. They can cause even more problems.

Relaxation methods

Initial insomniacs will find it beneficial to learn, and persevere with, some relaxation and meditation techniques. A form of hypnotherapy can

help here – see page 80. Remember, too, that you can use the hypnagogic (sleep-onset) state to help solve problems like this (see page 49).

The olfactory nerves in the nose lead to the limbic – or emotional – centre in the brain, and it has been established that certain aromas can have a calming effect. These include lemon balm, lavender, petitgram, neroli, frankincense, marjoram, camomile, clary sage, sandalwood, ylang ylang, mimosa and rosewood. Aromatherapy – in the form of massage with essential oils, a relaxing bath with fragrant oils or the use of aromatherapy candles – may prove useful for both types of stress-related insomnia.

Reducing stress and anxiety

Probably the single most effective treatment for insomnia is to eliminate stress. Examine what factors in your life tend to linger on in your thoughts and keep your brain busy, then try to do something about these sources of stress – strike a better balance in life.

Ensure that you allow enough time for yourself, and for the other aspects of your life that are important in the long run. Keep things in perspective – don't let problems that are trivial in the overall scheme of things assume undue significance.

Given that initial insomniacs tend to be rather too anxious, another technique is to address their specific fears and counter them. For instance, a person who worries about burglars and wakens frequently can remedy the situation by acquiring alarm equipment and locking the bedroom door.

Sometimes insomnia is dealt with through therapy, which involves trying to find out from the person's history when the insomnia started. It may be discovered that a specific event, such as the death of someone close, was linked to the onset of sleeplessness. Often in therapy the message simply has to be given to the unconscious that "it is all right now to stop suffering."

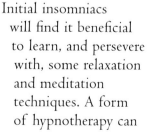

SWS PHENOMENA

Various sleep disorders – including sleepwalking, sleep-talking, teeth-grinding, bedwetting, sleep terrors and snoring – are linked to slow-wave sleep, or SWS (see page 39), in which muscular control is present (as distinct from REM sleep, when it is not). Because SWS is concentrated in the first half of the night, these problems are more likely to occur then, particularly within the first hour and a half of sleep, in other words, before the first REM period. In most cases nothing is recalled by the individual in the morning.

Sleepwalking

Somnambulism, commonly known as sleepwalking, occurs in Stage 4 slow-wave sleep. Episodes tend to last about 5–15 minutes, occasionally longer. It is usually impossible to attract the sleepwalker's attention. Normally they stay in the bedroom and get back into bed themselves, but they can be guided back into bed if necessary.

Sleepwalking seems to have a genetic component. It is especially common in children, peaking during adolescence. Stress appears to increase its frequency.

One amusing account was of a man who would get up in the night and busy himself tidying and cleaning the house. He had no memory of doing so and was convinced that his girlfriend was responsible. She was quite pleased with his amnesic nocturnal industry.

There have been some amazing tales of people sleepwalking long distances – even driving! It is clearly a dangerous condition and some cases of people falling from bedroom windows may well have been due to sleepwalking.

A practical approach for frequent sleepwalkers who might place themselves or others in physical danger is to fix an alarm on the bedroom door. Therapeutic techniques can also be helpful. One technique is to attempt to uncover and deal with whatever factor

Sleep terrors can be triggered by a sudden stimulus, such as a noise – so, for some people, earplugs may be the appropriate remedy!

Another type of sleep terror is where the individual imagines they are in a dangerous or frightening situation – perhaps reliving a trauma from their life. Thus, a former soldier, who had traumatic experiences in a minefield years before, would sometimes appear to wake and, kneeling on the bed, shout, "Don't move – there are mines here!"

Dr. Hearne, using hypnotherapy, dealt with a case where a husband was regularly attempting to strangle his wife in the night. The man was vividly imagining, in a sleep-terror situation, that he was being attacked, and he was retaliating. The wife had to move to another bedroom and the marriage was suffering great strain. The husband was dismissive of hypnotherapy, but one session turned out to be sufficient treatment. The technique used was to "reprogram" the husband so that as soon as he felt under attack he would instead recognize the situation as hallucinatory and unreal, and simply relax. You could try a similar approach using the therapeutic technique on page 79.

Snoring

Another condition associated with slow-wave sleep (in particular Stage 4), and hence the first part of the night's sleep, is snoring. This is caused by the soft palate at the back of the throat becoming relaxed so that a sonorous vibration occurs with breathing, especially when lying on one's back. Alcohol can exacerbate the problem as it increases the relaxation.

Snoring is not generally a problem for the snorer because he or she is oblivious to the sound, but it can cause considerable disturbance and annoyance to others in the vicinity – especially the bed-partner. The noise can be stentorian and has led to the break-up of many relationships.

A nose-clip may help if the air passage is significantly obstructed by the soft palate. An

operation may alleviate the condition, or hypnotherapy may be employed so that when the unconscious realizes that snoring is about to start, the body is caused to move, so lightening sleep. You can try this for yourself – see page 79.

OTHER SLEEP DISORDERS

Whereas the foregoing problems are mainly limited to slow-wave sleep, two other conditions – sleep apnoea and narcolepsy – are more generally disruptive.

Sleep apnoea

Sleep research has shown that some people who suffer from excessive daytime sleep do so because of a condition known as sleep apnoea. People with this condition actually stop breathing when they fall asleep, due to a disruption of the respiratory system or because of an obstruction in the upper tract.

Eventually, after a minute or so, the build-up of carbon dioxide in the blood causes an emergency waking response.

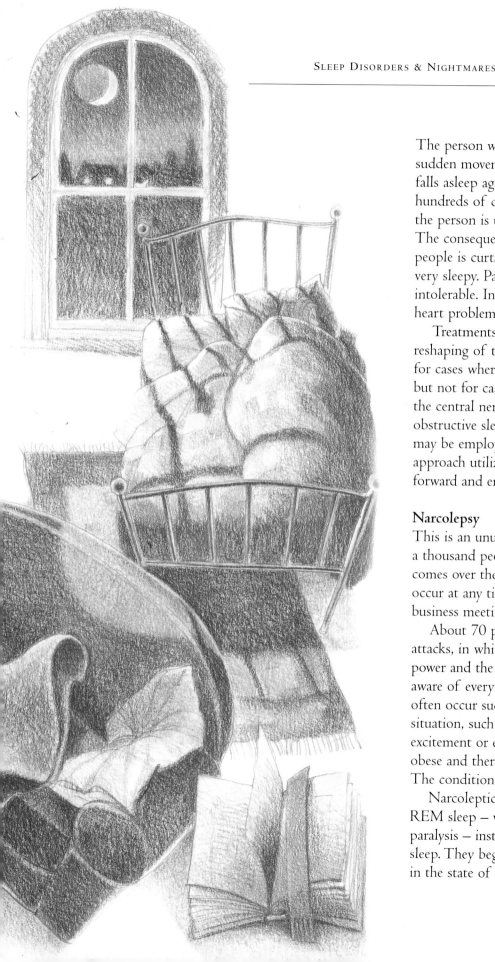

The person wakes briefly, perhaps making a big sudden movement, snorts or snores very loudly, then falls asleep again. The whole night consists of hundreds of dire-emergency automatic wakenings, but the person is unaware of what has been happening. The consequence is that the overall sleep of these people is curtailed, so that in the daytime they are very sleepy. Partners usually find sleeping with them intolerable. In severe cases sleep apnoea may lead to heart problems or stroke.

Treatments have included tracheotomy and partial reshaping of the soft palate. Such surgery is beneficial for cases where there is some form of airway blockage, but not for cases in which breathing is suppressed in the central nervous system. For severe cases of obstructive sleep apnoea, air pressure in a nasal mask may be employed to blow open the pharynx. Another approach utilizes a gum-shield that moves the jaw forward and enlarges the air space.

Narcolepsy

This is an unusual condition, affecting perhaps one in a thousand people, where an irresistible desire to sleep comes over the individual several times a day. It may occur at any time – for example, at a meal, during a business meeting or while talking to someone.

About 70 per cent of sufferers have "cataplectic" attacks, in which the muscles suddenly lose their power and the person collapses, unable to move yet aware of everything going on around. The attacks often occur suddenly as a result of an emotional situation, such as laughter, anger, amusement, excitement or even an orgasm. Sufferers are often obese and there seems to be a genetic factor involved. The condition mainly strikes first in the 20s or 30s.

Narcoleptics, when they fall asleep, go straight into REM sleep – with its accompanying muscular paralysis – instead of the various stages of slow-wave sleep. They begin to hallucinate, being simultaneously in the state of dreaming and wakefulness. The duration of these attacks is usually just a minute or two, although they can be as short as a few seconds or as long as an hour. Following an attack narcoleptics move into slow-wave sleep.

One woman reported: "I used to feel weak in the afternoons. I would fall on to the sofa and start to see things. I went to the doctor, who wrote a note to a psychiatrist saying I was displaying schizoid symptoms." This woman was actually misdiagnosed and labelled a schizophrenic. Unfortunately, because of ignorance by physicians, many narcoleptics are wrongly adjudged to be psychotic. However, there is a growing awareness of narcolepsy and various effective treatments have been developed.

REM NIGHTMARES

Some 96 per cent of reported nightmares are dreams occurring in REM sleep. In the sleep laboratory the signs of such an episode are obvious, which is not the case with slow-wave sleep terrors (see page 64). Heart-rate and breathing-rate measures increase over a few minutes. The sufferer sweats profusely and eventually bursts out of sleep – perhaps screaming – feeling extremely shocked and terrified. The threshing around often seen in films does not happen with REM nightmares, because, of course, the muscles are paralysed. And for the same reason, no amount of screaming in the dream will come through, until the moment of waking.

The American Charles Fisher conducted a sleep-laboratory study of nightmare sufferers. All seven subjects had been strongly traumatized and most had seen much violence in their homes when children. One 34-year-old woman developed a severe recurrent nightmare after a male intruder entered her apartment, threatened to strangle her, forced her to perform fellatio, then raped her. Her nightmares featured a train invading the room; a storm; a flow of hot lava; being choked by curtains; being in an elevator with the rapist; and screaming, with no one hearing.

Throughout the world, nightmares are a problem on a mammoth scale. Some unfortunate people experience bad dreams every night and a small proportion undergo torment, in the form of recurring nightmares, several times each night. These individuals dread going to sleep and are sometimes even driven to consider suicide.

It is likely that under certain circumstances nightmares can be responsible for deaths. It does not take a heart specialist to recognize the immense strain that frequent nightmares can place on the body's system. The threat to an individual suffering from a weak heart becomes very real, as the following case demonstrates:

> 66 *My nightmares are mostly about someone I knew years ago. During the nightmare I have uncompromising differences of opinion with him which develop into violent quarrels, to such an extent that I awake with severe chest pains reminiscent of my first heart attack. I am completely exhausted and find this very frightening in the middle of the night.* 99

Profile of the regular nightmare sufferer

Dr. Hearne made a special study of nightmares and the people who experience them. Of the 39 sufferers (of whom all but two were female), 90 per cent reported having recurring nightmares and in 70 per cent of those subjects the nightmares were on a repeating theme at least 70 per cent of the time. About 80 per cent stated that their nightmares started before the age of 20. Just over half thought that they began as a result of some trauma, such as sexual abuse. Because of the inevitable nightmares, 44 per cent had a fear of going to sleep. Among those who had tried various medications, all agreed they were ineffective.

In this study the most frequent *nightmare categories*, in descending order, were found to be:

- Witnessing horror or violence
- Experiencing attack or danger
- Flight from someone or something
- A sinister presence
- Being late and frustrated in travel
- Suffocation
- Hallucinated creatures
- Being paralysed

An average personality profile was computed for the sufferers from a psychometric test that measured 16 personality variables. This group of nightmare sufferers were found to be, overall, *affected by feelings, apprehensive, tense, undisciplined* and *self-sufficient*. This suggests that there is a particular type of person who will have nightmares.

We are all very different in how we react to situations. One person who is raped may have nightmares about it for the rest of their life, whereas another may be able to cope with and successfully come to terms with the assault. Regular nightmare sufferers tend to be anxious people, and so the effects of trauma may linger longer.

Physiological trigger

Strikingly, most subjects in the above study said that their nightmares happened between 2am and 4am –

in other words, during the first half of the night. This is a remarkable finding because most dreaming sleep is in the second half of the night.

Dr. Hearne believes that this unexpected anomaly indicates that REM nightmares have physiological rather than psychological causes – they are triggered because the dreamer is more "jumpy" in the first half of the night. As with sleep terrors, it may be that sudden noises initiate fear, which influences the dream. Indeed, some people report that their nightmares regularly occur at the same time of night. Perhaps an electrical timing device switches on at that point and the sound precipitates the event. One remedy may be the same as for sleep terrors – to use earplugs!

For Dr. Hearne's technique of dealing with nightmares by converting them to lucid dreams see page 101, and for David Melbourne's technique of interpretive therapy for nightmares see page 72.

Emotional content

Nightmares vary enormously, from the mildly disturbing to visions of terror. Invariably, they culminate in an emotional climax which usually wakens the dreamer. He or she will then spend much time – even days in some cases – going over the dream repeatedly. Occasionally, an aftertaste of these strong emotions can linger for years.

The majority of nightmares, when written down, will not appear at all frightening to a third party:

> 66 *I was at a garden party wearing my new dress. While shaking a lemonade bottle, a child leered at me. I just knew he was going to spray it all over me. I woke up feeling extremely distressed.* 99

In fact, rarely do monsters with evil intent appear in adults' nightmares, though they do feature in children's (see page 75). What makes a nightmare upsetting is the emotional content. Fear of the unknown is a common theme, as in the following dream:

> 66 *I found myself in a sort of basement with a door at the bottom of the stairs. As I approached, I became aware that something evil was waiting on the other side. I knew that I was supposed to open the door, but became so terrified that I turned and fled. I woke up, my heart pounding in my ears and in a sweat.* 99

If we consider this nightmare, we are dealing with nothing more than a basement and a door which, in itself, cannot be considered "nightmarish." The dreamer, however, obviously anticipated some sort of unseen evil lurking behind the door.

In dreams our emotions are often exaggerated. For instance, it is not unheard of for people to believe that they have witnessed the funniest event of their lives. Upon waking, however, recollection may invoke only a little mild amusement – especially as the dream begins to fade. Nevertheless, some nightmares do conform to the common notion that they are horrific, such as this example:

> 66 *A young man was being slowly crushed to death beneath a road roller. Blood gushed from his mouth and he was screaming. There was a loud crack as the machine crushed his head.* 99

the conscious mind. Some nightmares can begin as fairly mild recurring dreams, then over a period of time grow progressively more disturbing. This indicates that the subconscious – which is on duty 24 hours a day – sets out to alert us to something it has identified in our waking lives that needs some conscious attention or action. It seems that when these recurring dreams are ignored, they become more frequent and are accompanied by more unnerving content.

For example, a woman who sent in a nightmare for interpretation explained that several years earlier it had begun as a fairly gentle dream. However, as time passed, it grew progressively more frightening until she felt the need to find out the root cause through analysis. It transpired that she had allowed herself to be slowly embroiled in a situation where somebody had been taking advantage of her, to the extent that he was all but allowing her to support him financially.

Occasionally a recurring nightmare can display the reverse and gradually turn into a pleasant dream:

66 *Three times this nightmare was identical. The fourth, however, it wasn't exactly a nightmare anymore. Since then, it grew progressively less frightening, until the last time I had it, the dream had a pleasant ending.* 99

In this instance, the dreamer had identified and dealt with a situation in her life that, if allowed to develop, might have been damaging. In consultation, she realized that the transformation of the nightmare into an agreeable dream had coincided with her actions.

A small percentage of nightmares can dredge up painful memories buried in the past. This is particularly evident if the subconscious has identified a situation in the dreamer's life that resembles a past trauma. Sometimes the subconscious is using this association to warn the dreamer that a similar threat

Perhaps another example conforms even more accurately with most people's idea of true terror:

66 *I found myself alone in a graveyard at night. There was a full moon and I was frightened. I was very careful not to go near any of the gravestones. Then I saw a way out through a large pair of wrought-iron gates. In my hurry, I looked down to see that I was walking over a line of graves, which were clearly marked in the grass. I froze, desperately trying to find a way to the gates without treading on graves. Then a hand burst through the grass and gripped my ankle. As it began to pull me beneath the surface, I woke up in a terrible state.* 99

Messages from the subconscious

Through the authors' work on dream interpretation, it has become apparent that many of these powerful dreams are trying to impart some sort of message to might be looming on the horizon, in line with the precognitive function of many dreams (see page 53).

Similarly, something may happen, such as a news broadcast, which parallels traumatic circumstances from the dreamer's past. It acts like a trigger for the subconscious to concentrate its efforts on forcing the individual to face up to and deal with the pain from that trauma – hence the nightmares, or series of nightmares with recurring themes.

Symbolism and themes

Each dream is individual to the dreamer and might translate into an entirely different interpretation – depending on the personality and life circumstances of the subject. For example, a nightmare involving a graveyard, as described on page 71, might represent someone the dreamer knows who has died, or perhaps a fear of death – but equally, it could signify a disturbing event buried in the past, or something else completely different. This is why the notion of universal archetypal images (see page 31) simply does not hold water – because we do not have universally equivalent experiences.

Nevertheless, the following nightmare themes, by their nature, seem to point to some sort of past trauma or unpleasant incident: people leering and laughing at the dreamer, waving fists, swearing, behaving in a threatening manner, throwing things, pointing weapons, snarling and grunting, witnessing injury to others or seeing people in distress and pretending to be ignorant of the situation, and so on.

Interpretative therapy for nightmares

A large proportion of the dreams David Melbourne receives for interpretation are nightmares, and the majority of these are recurring. His experience in this field led him to develop his own technique of interpretative therapy to banish nightmares. He has effected cures, often with a single analysis, in people who have suffered from recurring nightmares for as

long as 15 years. Nowadays, depending on the circumstances, he combines his own method with Dr. Hearne's technique of utilizing the lucid dream (see page 101) and believes the only nightmares he cannot banish are those induced by certain medicinal drugs.

In order to build up a psychological profile of each subject, the authors have developed the "MHQ" (Melbourne–Hearne Questionnaire). Apart from providing a written account of the dream, this comprehensive four-page form provides a vast amount of detail about each dreamer, including age, usual occupation, date of birth, education, nationality, marital status, number of children, religion, interests and hobbies.

In addition, much information is gathered regarding the person's preoccupations and concerns at the time of the dream; significant anniversaries; whether the dreamer is introvert or extravert, assertive or mild, emotional or stable, trusting or suspicious; plus much more. The completed questionnaire reveals a clear picture of the subject's psychology and circumstances in life.

Therefore, the first stage of David Melbourne's method for curing nightmares begins by sending an MHQ, with a request to complete as much of it as possible. In doing so, the dreamer is compelled to write down the nightmare. This in itself seems to have a therapeutic effect, because the dreams usually become less frequent. Occasionally, David has discovered that the act of putting pen to paper and providing a detailed account of the dream itself results in a cure.

In psychology, facing up to pain can be a powerful weapon in the armoury of therapy, which is probably why forcing subjects to confront their pain by writing the dream down usually has a beneficial effect. Some sort of exorcism is apparently taking place. This is borne out by the fact that most of Melbourne's clients who have suffered from recurring nightmares seem to share a character trait whereby, rather than reflecting on the nightmare, they lean towards denial — in other words, they decide to put it out of their minds and not to dwell on it.

All this suggests that there is indeed a message that the subconscious wants the subject to acknowledge, albeit unconsciously. Nightmares, by their nature, force the dreamer to consider them over and over — sometimes throughout the following day. The act of thinking repeatedly about a nightmare will reduce the emotion of the original traumatic experience. This suggests that it is being exorcised, or the message of the dream is being understood.

However, although a minority of nightmares will be cured at this early stage, the majority persist in recurring, though less frequently. So the next step is to interpret the dream and reveal the hidden message — which is always present. This process can take several hours and requires a lot of careful study of the dream material, before conclusions can be reached. The dream has to be stripped down to its constituent parts, analysed, then reassembled again — all the time bearing in mind the information provided by the four-page questionnaire.

As a result of this detailed level of analysis, the root cause of the nightmare is revealed. This is then made known to the dreamer. Once this information is related to an ongoing problem or anxiety in the dreamer's life, the nightmares cease — a cure is effected.

A recurring nightmare

The following case from the authors' files provides a good example. It concerns Jan H., aged 37 years, who had the following recurrent nightmare.

> *I am my actual age, alone in an old house that has been added on to — it is known to me (not in real life), and there are narrow corridors on different levels. I find myself in a room with no windows, which is decorated lavishly in hues of dark red. Facing me, on one part of a wall, there is an arrangement of deep red, rich, velvety drapes. Apart from cushions on the floor, I am not aware of other furniture.*
>
> *Then, not knowing how I got there, I find myself in a corridor. I have been warned by somebody (who?) not to proceed further, yet I do. I notice windows through which there are shafts of sunlight. I can see shrubs in a sort of garden. Further down the corridor — around a corner — it is dark and gloomy, and feels forbidding and spooky. I feel afraid.*
>
> *I stop where the sunlight stops, where it becomes shadowy. At this point, I am very scared. Then I wake up, sweating, and afraid to go back to sleep.*

Additional comments that were made by the subject on the questionnaire were: "In the dream, I was sort of drifting" and "I thought the red room could be womb-like. Could some sort of renaissance be about to happen?"

Interpreting the nightmare

This is the interpretation of the nightmare, just as it was given to Jan H.:

To begin with, you state that in your dream you are your actual age. This alerts us to the fact that we are dealing with a current, ongoing situation in your life. The next clue comes when we study the house. Sometimes, a house can be a representation of ourselves. The attic, for example, may represent the mind; a bedroom could symbolize affairs of the heart, and so forth.

The fact that this house has been added on to alerts us that, in this instance, it is indeed a representation of you (the additions indicate lessons, experiences and perhaps knowledge that has been accrued throughout your life) – the scene, therefore, is set.

Next, you find yourself in a room where, your comments suggest, you feel fairly comfortable. The fact that it is lavishly decorated with warm red hues tends to support this hypothesis. In other words, this room represents the circumstances in your life with which you feel most comfortable. These areas are likely to be familiar, perhaps even encompassing a feeling of safety (suggested by your own observations concerning the womb).

The lack of windows suggests strongly that sometimes, to cope with life, you have a tendency towards denial, or not facing up to the need to "see" things in their true light – a temptation to bury your head in the sand, so to speak, in case certain consequences appear too horrible to contemplate. In this sense, the cushions suggest comfort, while the lack of furniture indicates a situation you might feel is not permanent (could change at any time). This signifies that although you are able to turn in on yourself now, you fear what the future might hold.

Now we come to the crux of the dream, and one that reinforces the entire interpretation. You state that

you seem to drift around, and this remark is very relevant. It reflects your feelings in day-to-day living – you feel that instead of having control of your affairs, you are perhaps being carried along on the prevailing current. Then you find yourself in one of the corridors (an optional new route to travel in life).

However, you are warned not to proceed, but by whom? Clearly this is a message from your subconscious, and soon we see the reason why. At the end of this corridor (representing an optional new route in life), where there is a sort of turning or

corner, there is darkness (no windows again).

So here we have a clear message, and one which, to bring an end to these nightmares, needs to be acted upon. Your subconscious has identified an ongoing problem in your life which, although you acknowledge its existence, you tend not to look at or dwell on. In other words, you either turn a blind eye (no window), or pretend for a while that it does not exist.

Your subconscious is pointing out that there is a way out of this dilemma, providing that you face up to and "look at" the options (keep yourself in the light). If you proceed to take action while at the same time not acknowledging the possible consequences (keeping yourself in the dark), your situation could go from bad to worse.

So here we have a recurring dream that is screaming a message at you! Whatever you do, do not continue in a state of denial (darkness). You simply have to face up to things and deal with them — stay in the light and acknowledge where you are heading and the possible consequences.

The shrubs in the garden outside represent your way out (into the light). Therefore, it is likely that you will see the light (the right way out of your problem), but might still be tempted back into the shadows — this should be resisted. As the consistent theme of the dream concerns being in the dark or shadows, this could also indicate that, to a certain extent, something

or somebody in your life could be preventing you from having your own opinion regarding the problem. In this respect, you should insist that your views are brought to light and aired in the open (the garden).

This nightmare highlights the point made earlier, that, to a third party, such dreams rarely appear frightening. What is important is how the subject perceives the content of the dream which, in turn, shows up as powerful emotions.

CHILDREN AND REM NIGHTMARES

Most people will have memories of nightmares during childhood. In fact, to a large extent, the cursed territory of the nightmare seems to abide with children. These bad dreams often feature from early childhood until the onset of puberty. Unlike adult

nightmares, they are far more likely to feature
monsters and vicious-looking creatures, although the
emotion still depends on how the child perceives these
dreams. Being pursued or experiencing a sense of
imminent danger are other common themes.

Recurring themes in children's nightmares
In childhood, nightmares can also have a recurring
theme, but there is a straightforward technique for
dealing with this. Children are particularly
susceptible to the power of hypnotic suggestion,
especially during the hypnagogic (sleep-onset) state
or if they have just awoken. Therefore, if a child is
given to recurring nightmares, a parent can employ a
method very closely allied to Dr. Hearne's technique
of converting a nightmare to a lucid dream (see
page 101).

After putting these vulnerable children to bed, the
parent should stay with them. As they begin to show
symptoms of becoming sleepy and entering the
hypnagogic state, the parent should begin making
positive suggestions along the following lines:

*I don't think you'll have a bad dream tonight. In fact, I know
that they're going to get better. But if you do, all you have to do is
to magic (or conjure) Mummy and Daddy into your dream, and
they will make sure that it never bothers you again. Mummy and
Daddy will make sure that nothing hurts you! Mummy and
Daddy will keep you safe.*

If the child wants to know how you will manage this,
ask them how they would like to see you deal with it.
This is likely to invoke positive visual imagery that
will reinforce the suggestion. In fact, what is
happening here is that the child is being programmed
to initiate temporary lucidity – long enough to
conjure Mummy or Daddy into the dream to cope
with whatever threat there may be.
    Children are also likely to respond to the Native
American "dream catcher" – it is supposed to filter

the dreams, which are believed to descend from the night sky, so that only good dreams are allowed through to the dreamer (see page 24).

Children's one-off nightmares

A good technique to employ for the occasional one-off nightmare – when the child has already been frightened awake – involves some play-acting on the part of the parent, often to the amusement of the partner. However, it is a very effective method to prevent a child from slipping back into a disturbing dream.

When a child wakes up screaming, get to them as quickly as possible. Reassure them and persuade them to tell you about the object of their fear. For example, they may respond by sobbing, "The monster was coming after me!"

At that point a parent should leap into action. Tell the child that you heard the monster, creature, man, or whatever, outside the door.

Then pretend to chase after it and catch it, within the child's hearing. If, for example, there are two parents present, it does not matter if the ensuing grunts and sounds of a mock battle give rise to laughter – it is a positive response, and one that is likely to instil even more confidence in the child.

After the monster has been killed or vanquished and the parent has returned puffing and panting, a brief description of how he or she turned the creature inside out and threw it at least a hundred miles away, should be given. After all, if Mummy or Daddy can't deal with it, who else can?

If we analyse the psychology behind this successful technique, it becomes clear that if children sincerely believe that the object of their fear has been destroyed, it is hardly likely to present itself in a nightmare ever again – a permanent end to that particular monster!

THERAPEUTIC TECHNIQUES FOR SLEEP PROBLEMS

Many of the sleep problems described in this section can be alleviated or cured by a straightforward therapeutic technique that involves giving definite suggestions to the sufferer. The suggestions seem to act like instructions to the unconscious mind so that when the sleep problem starts, it is immediately recognized and an alternative behaviour substituted that overrides the problem.

Use the following scripts to make these suggestions to the sufferer. Use the "initial relaxation script" first in order to induce a relaxed frame of mind and then follow it with either the all-purpose therapeutic "script" or one of the scripts for dealing with insomnia and sleep paralysis, which can be read to the sufferer once they are relaxed. If you are the sufferer, get someone to read it to you, or make your own recording of the script and listen to it yourself.

Initial relaxation script
If possible, read the following script just before the person who has the sleep problem goes to sleep. Read it slowly and pause for a few seconds each time at the dots.

Close your eyes and relax each part of your body in turn, starting at your toes. Wiggle your toes and relax your feet. . . . Focus your attention now on your ankles and calf muscles and allow them to relax. . . . Sense that relaxation spreading to your thigh muscles . . . now to your abdomen . . . and chest. Take a deep breath and now focus on your shoulders — feel those muscles relax. . . . Now sense that relaxation spreading down your arms . . . to your hands and the tips of your fingers. . . . Now relax the muscles in your neck . . . and face . . . and forehead . . . and scalp.

All-purpose script
After following the relaxation script, recite these next instructions two or three times so that they are fully understood and they register strongly. Insert the person's problem — sleepwalking, sleep-talking, teeth-grinding, feeling panicky, snoring, and so on — at the relevant parts in this script; sleepwalking is used as an example here. Remember to pause at the dots.

There is a deep part of your mind . . . your unconscious . . . which has the power to affect your body . . . and is aware of everything that is happening . . . even when you are asleep. . . . Now I want to communicate with that deep part of you . . . and ask for its help in stopping the problem . . . that you experience in sleep . . . because you do not want it to happen anymore. . . . Your unconscious is able to reprogram your behaviour in sleep . . . so that whenever you are about to sleepwalk . . . you will move, turn over, stop sleepwalking and relax into restful sleep again. You will do this automatically . . . unless you detect a genuine state of external or internal emergency . . . when waking will occur. . . . (I will repeat these instructions. . . .)

See how well the person responds to these direct suggestions. In some people who respond well initially, it may be necessary to "top up" the instructions from time to time.

Return to pre-suggestion state
To return the person to the pre-suggestion state after using a script, simply say to them the following words:

On the count of three you will be fully alert again, with eyes open. One, two, three, eyes open!

Dealing with sleep terrors
If you or someone you know is prone to sleep terrors (see page 64), use the initial relaxation script and then the all-purpose script, inserting the following wording for sleepwalk(ing): *react(ing) with anger or fear to a situation when your unconscious knows that you are really safely asleep.*

Countdown for insomnia

To deal with insomnia (see page 60), recite the initial relaxation script and then read the following script two or three times, remembering to pause at the dots:

Each time you go to bed in order to sleep . . . I want you to very slowly count down . . . from ten to one, and with each descending number . . . you will feel . . . deeper and deeper relaxed . . . and this will also push any anxieties and worries . . . further and further away . . . so that soon after . . . you have counted down to one . . . you will automatically drift into a wonderful . . . deep . . . sleep . . . which will be so good for your bodily health . . . state of mind . . . and sense of well-being. . . . That exquisite sleep state will last for the whole night . . . and in the morning . . . you will awaken . . . feeling fully refreshed . . . and on top of the world. . . .

 Now, there is a deep part of your mind . . . your unconscious . . . which has the power to affect your body . . . and is aware of everything that is happening . . . even when you are asleep . . . I want now to communicate with that deep part of you . . . and ask for its help. . . . If it detects that you are about to wake up before it is appropriate for you to awaken . . . you will instantly override the awakening and re-introduce deep, restful sleep . . . unless there is a genuine emergency . . . when waking will occur . . . (I will repeat these instructions . . .)

To return the person to the pre-suggestion state, simply say to them the words shown under "Return to pre-suggestion state."

Dealing with sleep paralysis

If someone suffers from this condition – of seeming to wake up yet being quite unable to move (see page 49) – it is useful simply to practise the following scenario so that you will know what to do when it happens suddenly. Precede it with the initial relaxation script, then repeat the following script two or three times, pausing at the dots:

Imagine now awakening from a dream . . . and finding yourself unable to move. . . . Instantly I want you to think this is sleep paralysis. . . . It is a natural effect. . . . Your mind has woken . . . yet your body is still in dreaming sleep . . . and is therefore paralysed . . . so that you don't hurt yourself by acting out your dreams. . . . Consider how clever the body is . . . to protect you in this way. . . . It doesn't affect your breathing, because that is automatic anyway. . . . Your body is looking after you. . . . You know that everything is perfectly safe . . . and that sometimes even . . . the dream may make you think that strangers are nearby . . . but it is only a dream. . . . Enjoy the experience. . . . Wonder at the subtlety of nature . . . and simply allow yourself to relax . . . and drift back into a dream . . . from which you know you will awaken later . . . quite naturally . . . You simply have to relax. . . . (I will repeat what I have said. . . .)

Again, to return the person to the pre-suggestion state, simply say to them the words shown under "Return to pre-suggestion state."

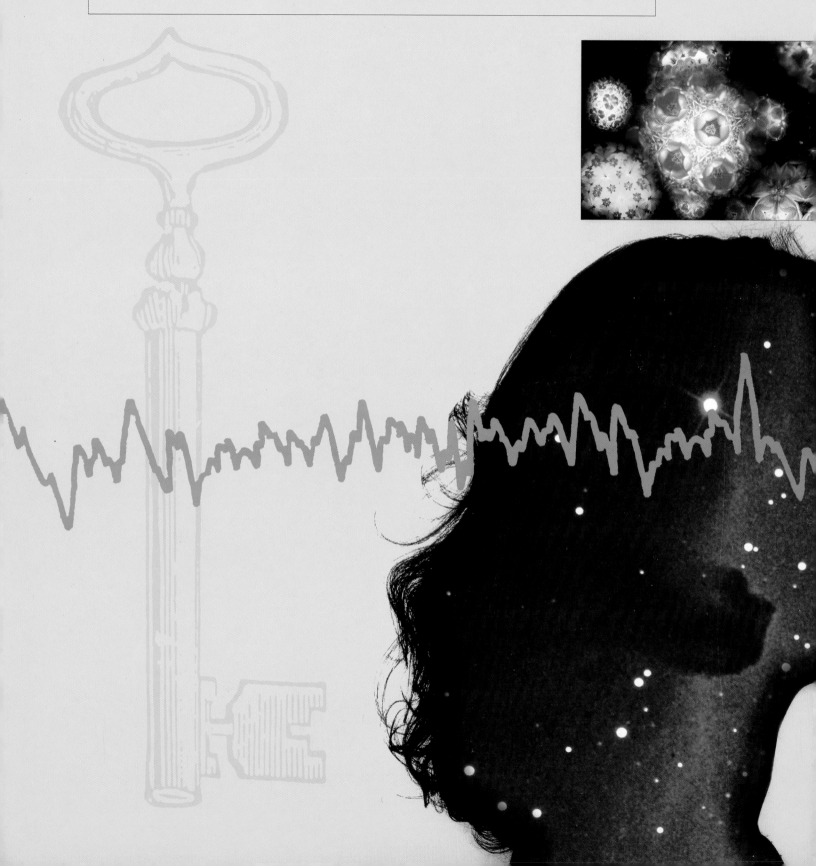

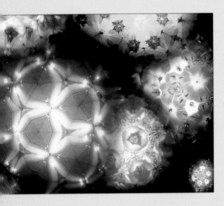

Several areas of dream research that the authors are exploring allow access to new areas of psychological understanding. The study of lucid dreams, in which dreamers recognize that they are dreaming and learn to control their dreams, offers enormous potential for self-discovery and life-enhancement. Lucid dreams can be induced in various ways, including the use of "false awakenings" and nightmares as springboards into the lucid dream, and methods for teaching yourself to do this are included here. Another technique that has provided much insight into the nature of dreams is "dream tracing,"

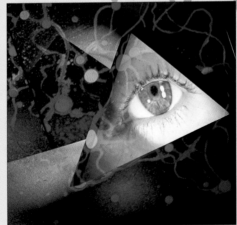

which allows the viewing of mental imagery from hypnotically induced dreams. This has led to exciting developments in psychotherapy techniques.

THE LUCID DREAM: A PROVEN PHENOMENON

Perhaps the most astounding discovery in the field of dream research is that of the lucid dream, in which the dreamer knows they are dreaming. This was proved to be a real phenomenon in 1975 when Dr. Hearne established the first structured communication from a lucid dreamer (within a dream) to the outside world (see page 34). The experiment also established for the first time that we do indeed dream – until then, all claims that dreams were real had to be regarded as purely anecdotal. Nowadays, universities all over the world are studying the subject of lucid dreaming.

Surprisingly, more than 20 years after the publication of these findings, many psychologists still believe that it is impossible for somebody to be fully conscious – in every sense – yet also be dreaming. Nevertheless, it is proven fact. Incredible as it sounds, lucid dreamers have both long- and short-term memory and full conscious awareness of their identity restored. They are wide awake, but inside a dream.

Levels of lucidity

The level of lucidity achieved within a dream, however, varies considerably from person to person. Therefore, in order to make the phenomenon better understood, we have categorized levels of lucidity, which fall broadly into four groups:

Slight lucidity: This is the most common and occurs when, for a fleeting moment, subjects become aware that they are dreaming, before lapsing into a conventional dream. This sometimes happens during nightmares.

Medium lucidity: A smaller proportion of the population can be conscious that they have achieved full long-and-short term memory (regained their identity), but take no active part in the dream. Instead, they observe in wonderment, as the dream unfolds around them.

Good lucidity: A still smaller number of people are fortunate enough not only to find their memory and identity restored, but also to be able to take an active part in the dream. These individuals are capable of learning how to influence, manipulate and, ultimately, control the events of the dream.

Full-blown lucidity: Finally, there are a few people who are able to experience an even more astounding condition: based on the reports received, it appears they are able to utilize the lucid dream to initiate an out-of-body experience (see page 101).

The lucid-dreaming experience

It is impossible to find words that will come close to describing a powerful degree of lucidity within a dream. A large proportion of lucid dreamers become more spiritual in their outlook. In fact, the experience can be so overwhelming, it can change one's entire outlook on life itself.

In addition to possessing the astounding awareness of being conscious yet in a dream environment, another amazing feature of a lucid dream is the fact that the dreamer can actually control what happens by mere thought. Essentially, they think something and then it happens.

If lucid dreamers wish to fly, they can fly. If they think of a specific individual – even a deceased relative – that person will almost certainly appear. Deceased family members will appear so palpable that when lucid dreamers awaken, they wonder whether they have actually met the authentic relative.

Levels of reality

Whether they are flying, making love or talking to a long-lost soul, the experience will be so convincing that it will not be discernible from the reality of this existence. Indeed, most lucid dreamers are so overwhelmed with the actuality of the situation that they are convinced they are in another level of reality – and who is to say they are not?

To undergo such a potent degree of lucidity, therefore, raises the all-important question: is the lucid dream another level of reality, and is reality as we know it just another dream state? In other words, can both conditions be regarded as interchangeable?

In turn, these questions raise other issues. If the lucid dream is indeed another level of reality, as the evidence suggests, then Dr. Hearne's theory that we all exist in a mentalistic universe – an interactive universe created by the mind – becomes feasible.

Dr. Hearne is obviously not the first person to have conjectured that the material world might be an illusion. The ancient Chinese sage Chuang Tzu, for example, said: "While men are dreaming they do not perceive that it is a dream. Some will even have a dream within a dream. And so when the great awakening comes upon us, shall we know this life to be a great dream. Only fools believe themselves to be awake now."

Firsthand account

Mark Creed, a lucid dreamer involved in our research programme, here gives an account of one of his lucid dreams, illustrating how convincing this dream world can be:

> ❝ *I was dreaming of my primary school. I was in the playground running around, trying to remember what it was like. It was so real that it was exactly how it was 30 years ago. I ran up the hill near the infants' building, then under the trees. I noticed the leaves on the ground, but it wasn't quite as it used to be, so I adjusted it, making the trees larger to give more shade.*
>
> *As I gazed down at the junior section of the school, I thought, 'Hang on, this is a dream!' Then I made a point of concentrating hard so that I would stay conscious. At this point, everything was startlingly real, though I knew that it was a dream.*
>
> *I ran down to the gate, opened it and went out on to the road – aware and conscious of every detail.*

Immediately, I recalled that David Melbourne and Dr. Hearne had asked me to carry out certain experiments. Accordingly, I remembered that I needed to see someone with a view to asking them something about the future. I felt sure that there was somebody specifically whom I wanted to conjure up, but was unable to recall who. By this time, I was thinking absolutely clearly, on a par with waking consciousness — and was aware of it.

I remembered with clarity agreeing with David that the next lucid dream I had, I should ask somebody about a future event. However, it then occurred to me that I hadn't made any advance plans to conjure up anybody specific and, for a moment, my mind was blank. I really couldn't think of anyone at a moment's notice.

I ran down the road, Smith's Field on the left, approaching the Harpers' house on the right. There wasn't a soul about, and I was desperate to ask somebody about the future. I gazed down the road to see that it was empty (which would be normal), and I realized that I would be unlikely to meet anybody.

My only hope was the Harpers, and as I ran down towards the house, I saw the back door open (on cue). Their house hasn't changed much over the years, but it was exactly how it used to be, even down to the old back door.

Although nobody came out, the opened door told me that somebody was in. Despite the fact that I knew this was all a dream, it was so stunningly real, I felt I needed an excuse to visit — I just couldn't go barging in even though I knew that anybody inside would be the product of my dream. I didn't want to offend them. Then, right on cue again, it started to rain, in fact it became a deluge, just the excuse I needed — to shelter from the rain.

I ran through the gate to the door and knocked. Voices shouted, 'Come in.' I stepped over the threshold and into the kitchen. Norman and Anne Harper were there in the flesh. So too was their daughter, Alison. I asked if I could shelter from the rain, to which they replied, 'Of course, come in.'

I looked down to see that I was now wearing my waterproofs which were bone dry. I wondered how this could be, as it was pouring down outside. I looked up and studied the kitchen, which was small and old-fashioned. On the side were two televisions which looked very similar to old radios. One had a very small, almost round, black-and-white picture, while the other was a normal-sized black-and-white image — both pictures were very clear.

Norman, Anne and Alison were pleased to see me, and I was pleased to see them, too. I was itching to ask them to tell me

something about the future, but the reality and ordinariness of the situation made me feel too embarrassed to ask. They might think I was nuts. Despite the fact that everything was so real and I was thinking clearly, I actually felt quite silly and decided to wait and pick the right moment.

Anne asked me if I would like a cup of tea. I said yes, and she went to the cooker. I had a good look at it — an old-fashioned gas stove. She picked up the kettle, filled it with water and put it on the cooker.

I stood trying to pick the moment to ask about the future. It just felt so awkward to put such a silly question to people I know and I actually thought, 'I won't ask now, I'll wait a little longer.' At that point, I woke up and looked at the clock — it was 5.20am. I felt good. **"**

After considering his dream, Mark made some further observations:

" The whole dream had a nostalgic feel to it. The initial memories were from 30 years ago, and the inside of the Harpers' house was old-fashioned. I am unable to remember if it was an accurate replica of the original building. The dream was very lucid and I had all my faculties about me. Although I knew it was a dream, I felt the need to behave politely to the Harpers (as I would in reality). I felt embarrassed and silly as I tried to pick the moment to ask about the future.

There is no doubt that the full gamut of emotions, feelings and behaviours are switched on in a lucid dream. I found that it really is extraordinarily difficult to act contrary to my nature, even when I know that I can do anything I want.

I can hardly believe I didn't ask about the future. It seems so pathetic now. I get caught up in the reality of it all so much that I really am beginning to think that if a lucid dream was able to continue indefinitely, I would forget it was a dream and live it as if it was reality. **"**

Typical features

Mark's experience invites some interesting observations. First, it is clear that his dream was extremely vivid. Then, just after he had altered the size of the trees (an impossible anomaly in reality), he realized he was dreaming. He then concentrated hard to remain lucid, at which point everything became startlingly real.

The fact that he recalled the experiments we had asked him to do, and then set out to complete them, demonstrates the powerful level of lucidity – he began to take an active, conscious role in the dream. Interestingly, he needed an excuse to enter the Harpers' house, and then, lo and behold, it started raining (the power of expectancy).

The unusual placement of two televisions together – both switched on – introducing another anomaly, might have been a device that his subconscious used to prolong lucidity. Mark recalled how unusual they appeared, and commented that the quality of pictures being televised was too good for the era.

What is fascinating is that everything was so real that Mark was unable to act out of character with people he once knew – for fear of ridicule. Also interesting is Mark's speculation about becoming part of that reality if it continued indefinitely – this could not be achieved in a conventional dream. The awareness in conventional dreams is nothing like that of lucid dreams, which have much in common with waking reality.

Amassing evidence

Since Mark first started experiencing lucid dreams, he has become one of a group of regular lucid dreamers who endeavour to assist our research by conducting certain experiments for us. Through this research we hope one day to amass enough evidence to be statistically significant in certain areas, among which are prodromic dreams (forewarning of illness), healing dreams, stress control, grief therapy, precognition,

creativity, learning and discovering consistent effects – to name only a few.

Sue Whittaker, a new lucid dreamer and recruit to our research programme, is currently trying to establish what happens when she attempts to pass through solid objects in a lucid dream. This is important research and, like the light-switch effect (see page 35), may reveal important connotations in the field of dream interpretation.

For example, it would appear that it is more difficult to pass through certain solid objects than others. If this is true, then it will affect the interpretation of the dream. A report of a dream where, say, a person experienced difficulty handling or interacting with certain materials might be incorrectly interpreted if the analyst were ignorant of the effect and attributed it to the character of the dreamer.

Sue Whittaker describes her first experiment in this area in the following account:

> ❝ I dreamt that I woke up in a strange room and remembered to say, 'This is a lucid dream.' I found myself flying. I remembered that David Melbourne had asked me to carry out some experiments for him. He wanted me to see if I could pass through solid objects.
>
> I thought, 'Here goes!' I was in the 'Superman' position, arms stretched out in front of me. I was flying at speed, straight towards the opposite wall. I managed to put my hands through it, then the dream ended and I woke up. It was as if I wasn't allowed to do that. Perhaps I will be allowed to go a bit further next time.
>
> I woke up with a migraine that lasted the whole day. I get migraines when I've been overdoing things, although I haven't had one for months. Maybe it has something to do with hitting a solid wall at speed! ❞

Sue Whittaker's experience provides a good example of how a novice lucid dreamer can be so enthusiastic and overwhelmed by the event that lucidity can slip away. Sue's case also raises another question – can the effects of lucid-dreaming occurrences be carried over into the waking world, in the form of physical manifestations?

THE REALM OF THE EXTRAORDINARY

Exhilarating activities and bizarre experiences often occur in lucid dreams, which the dreamer can learn to control.

New heights
Sue Whittaker's abruptly curtailed flight notwithstanding, flying can be an extremely pleasurable activity for the lucid dreamer. Some people simply flap their arms gently in the dream and take off effortlessly, while others zoom like a rocket, or just float. It is surprising that such imagery is produced so easily, since in wakefulness we do not usually experience aerial views of places and so are not greatly familiar with them. The scenes can be truly spectacular and awe-inspiring, as this account reveals:

> ❝ I have flown, or rather soared at great heights, viewing scenes and areas of the world I have not seen, but have read about or perhaps viewed on television. In my dreams I am able to float down to any place I choose. I am always dressed in white apparel which is of a cloudy appearance. My arms do not flap but are able to move about quite naturally while I am in the air. To leave the ground, my arms are always extended above my head, with the palms of my hands touching. ❞

in a red satin shirt with a bandana round his head, and had brilliant blue trousers. He looked very proud and regal. He smiled, and in his eyes and smile it seemed that I had found eternal peace, joy, tranquillity and love. I realized that I was a peasant maiden, as I was dressed in clothes of years ago. It was a very intensely emotional and beautiful dream, and I knew throughout it was a dream. 99

Experimentation

People who are used to lucid dreaming quite often experiment and notice interesting effects, as in the following account:

66 I realized the absurdity of using a pedestrian crossing in a dream when I was not in a material form. Presumably, as I was not solid, a vehicle could pass harmlessly through the space which I was occupying, or I could pass through the vehicle. I decided to test this idea in the most extreme way I could think of, which was to attempt to travel through someone else in the dream. I selected a passer-by at random and, moving horizontally, aimed myself at a point just beneath the ribs. My experience was entirely unexpected: on entry, vision stopped but I felt, with a fairly lifelike intensity, sensations of warmth and moisture. These lasted only a second or two, then I emerged the other side of the body. 99

The woman recording the following lucid dream had an exquisitely beautiful experience:

66 I was floating up what seemed a never-ending bright green hill, dressed in long rainbow-coloured clothes, barefoot, with flowing hair. It was a warm day and it seemed as if everywhere was filled with warm yellow sunshine. I saw a rider on horseback on the hilltop. He saw me and rode down. As he came closer, he pulled up the horse's reins and the horse reared on its back legs (like in the films). I saw that the rider was handsome, with a compelling face. He looked like a cross between a gypsy and a pirate and was dressed

The pleasure the dreamer takes in being in control of events is evident in the following account:

> *When I become aware that I am dreaming, I try to do silly things to see if I can make them happen, like flying and walking through walls. Once when I was 15, I even managed to beat up a school bully. There was a lot of satisfaction in that.*

Sexual encounters

Sexual activity is quite often reported in lucid dreams. Some lucid dreamers engineer sexual situations using dream control. With this subject the situation was literally forced upon him:

> *I went for a walk within my old school as I remembered it. A tennis teacher asked me to wait, as I passed the courts. She ran up to me and kissed me. I was certain that this, being too good to be true, would waken me — but it did not. She was wearing a white skirt and singlet, with white socks and plimsolls. She pulled me down on top of her on to the grass. I remember that people were walking past and took no notice of us and tennis continued on the adjacent courts. We made love and I even orgasmed inside her, in full, and felt the ejaculation. At that point I awoke.*
>
> *It was a complete and yet very sad dream — because it was a very beautiful experience and I knew I could never know who she was or see her again. She was so very real. Incidentally, I did not have a 'wet' dream — though the sensation was real enough.*

This last point shows how cerebral sex is in humans. There was a full orgasm psychologically with a feeling of ejaculation, but none occurred in reality.

CONJURING POTENTIAL

The key to controlling lucid dreams is to remember that what you think, you will then dream. If you would like to see and talk to a deceased uncle, for example, you would consciously wish that you could see him (while you are dreaming), then you would cover or close your (dream) eyes for a moment. When you uncovered or opened them again, the likelihood is that your uncle would be standing in front of you.

An engineer could conjure up a technician, who might show him how to solve a particular engineering problem. Jack Nicklaus, the famous golfer, improved his game immensely after being shown in a lucid dream how to change his grip.

Likewise, employing the same technique, you could will yourself to another location. It could be a tropical beach for a romantic liaison, a famous racing circuit where you will be competing or a hospital where you are administering healing – nothing is ruled out.

Creative opportunities

For those who are creative, the lucid dream presents a wonderland of opportunity. A person who is interested in art, for instance, could conjure up a gallery packed full of fabulous paintings created by the subconscious. The most stunning one could then be memorized, to be duplicated upon waking.

Perhaps a musician could witness the performance of new, spectacular musical compositions, which could be brought back to the material world. In fact, Dr. Hearne and psychologist Robin Furman have already been inspired in dreams to produce such compositions. Dr. Hearne's piece entitled "Walk to the Pagoda" (see photograph below) is based on music heard in a dream. Robin Furman's piece "Dream Theme" was also heard in a dream and written down on waking. Paul McCartney has told how he

Your subconscious is on duty 24 hours a day and will be aware of your goal. It is likely then that this repetitive behaviour will trigger a dream in which you find yourself gazing at your fingernails. However, because your subconscious knows your plan, it is likely to present you with an outlandishly different set of fingernails – they could be heart-shaped, for instance.

Because you will have developed the ritualistic behaviour of studying your nails in waking life, and concentrated your efforts on initiating a lucid dream, the difference should be noticed as an impossible anomaly in the dream. You are then likely to say to yourself, "These aren't my nails – I must be dreaming." The moment you recognize that you are in a dream, lucidity will follow.

Lucid-dream induction script
Hypnotherapy techniques can often be very successful at helping a dreamer to recognize anomalies and thus induce lucid dreaming. If you wish to try this, follow the instructions on page 79 for therapeutic techniques. Start with the initial relaxation script on that page, followed by the lucid-dream induction script given here. Repeat the script slowly two or three times, remembering to pause at the dots, then return to the pre-suggestion state as directed on page 79.

Tonight . . . when you are asleep and dreaming . . . something in the dream . . . will make you begin to realize . . . that you are dreaming. . . . It may be perhaps . . . that someone's face . . . will look different from how you know that person to be . . . or possibly . . . their clothes. . . . They may be wearing something . . . that you know they would never wear. . . . Or perhaps a familiar room . . . may have something different about it. . . . At that moment of recognition . . . of a fault in the dream picture . . . you will become excited . . . and say to yourself . . . 'This is a dream . . . . I am aware I am dreaming. . . . It is a lucid dream." . . . And you will remember . . . that you can control the dream's activities . . . to your advantage. . . . In the lucid dream . . . you can travel anywhere you want. . . . You can fly . . . or cover your eyes and think of a place where you would like to be . . . then, opening your eyes . . . find yourself there. . . . You can meet anyone you want in the dream . . . for instance, by opening a door . . . and willing them to be there. . . . You can do anything you want. . . . (I will repeat these instructions. . . .)

If these methods do not bring results, you could try combining the techniques – willing yourself back into the dream, and introducing an anomaly, with or without using the script. Of course, you may still encounter failure – but all is not lost, as there are other ways of cracking this sometimes-hard nut. One method that frequently works is to try to induce a so-called "false awakening" and then utilize that to create a lucid dream.

The nature of false awakenings

A major clue to a false awakening is the "light-switch effect" (see page 35). You may try to switch on a bedside lamp and it won't work, or you go to the bathroom and find that the light there doesn't work. If you perform such a test and suspect that you are actually still dreaming, you can test further by, say, jumping off something. If you find yourself floating down, then clearly you are dreaming. With that awareness you can walk through walls, explore your locality and so forth. The condition will end spontaneously after a while.

> " *I 'woke up' in my bedroom and looked around. It was an ordinary wakening and the room was clear although the imagery was not bright. I could hear other members of the family about the house. When I tried to switch on the bedside light, though, nothing happened. I thought, 'Oh well, the bulb has gone.' I got out of bed, put on my robe and went to the bathroom. I looked out of the window and discovered to my amazement that the road was not at all as it really is. The surprise woke me up properly.* "

Sometimes false awakenings follow on from an unpleasant dream, as if the illusion of waking is a means of escape:

> " *I had just come home from an evening out and was fully clothed, when I heard a noise in my daughter's bedroom. I went to investigate. The room was different and a man was there wearing leather headgear with studs on it. He was chained. He went berserk and tried to get free but could not do so, and started crying. I said I could help him to get free but as I started to assist him, he struggled wildly again, so I ran from the room.*
>
> *I ran into my own room, jumped on the bed and my daughter woke up and asked me what was the matter. I told her I'd just had a bad dream. She asked what happened and I pointed out to the other bedroom. I looked at the wall*

INDUCING LUCID DREAMS THROUGH FALSE AWAKENINGS

You may be familiar with "false awakenings," where you appear to have woken and everything is quite normal – your bedroom is exactly as it should be and you go about the home – but at some point you see something so impossible that you realize you are dreaming and suddenly wake up. This extremely convincing false-awakening phenomenon can be very disorienting. It is related to lucid dreaming, because the dreamer's thinking is clear and logical, but in this case the realization of dreaming is lacking. Often a lucid dream will convert into a false awakening – or you can use a false awakening to induce a lucid dream.

as I pointed and then ducked in time as a hail of bullets came through the wall. I felt the bullets whizz past my head. 'Phew,' I said to my daughter calmly, 'that was a near thing.' I then turned over on to my left side and woke up. I then realized the whole thing had been a dream!

Occasionally, multiple false awakenings are reported:

I am a nurse and I dreamt I was sleeping and had wakened on hearing what I thought was one of the nursing officers. I dived across the room, knocking over tables and chairs. Then I heard voices at the door and the door being locked. I then knew I was dreaming and decided to wake up. What I did not realize was that I 'woke' into another dream, and when I stood up everything was lying on the floor as it was in my first dream. The door was locked, so I began banging on it and shouting to get out. My relief nurse and another nurse unlocked the door. Shortly afterwards, I really woke up.

When excessive, multiple false awakenings become totally disconcerting:

It was a lovely morning when I awoke, to get up for school. I got up, washed and changed, had breakfast and waited for the school bus. I was chatting to friends, when there was a bang, and I woke up. I got up, washed, changed, had breakfast, caught the bus and arrived at school. During registration a boy threw a book which hit me on the head, and I woke up! This time, I got up, washed, changed, etc., got to school, had my lessons and was having break, when my mother woke me up! I rushed to get ready for school, told my friends at school all that had happened and everything went fine until dinner time, when the school fire-alarm went off. There was panic, someone stumbled over me and I hurt my leg. I woke up in bed – it was dark and the clock showed 2am. Was I still asleep? It was not until bedtime the next night that I really knew and believed that I was awake.

Types of false awakening

In her book *Lucid Dreams*, published in 1968, the British writer Celia Green categorized two forms of false awakening, which she called Type 1 and Type 2. An example of a Type 1 false awakening, cited by Green, is from Dr. Frederik van Eeden (see page 33), who recorded his lucid dreams in the early part of the twentieth century:

I had a lucid dream in which I made the following experiment. I drew with my finger, moistened by saliva, a wet-cross on the palm of my left hand, with the intention of seeing whether it would still be there after waking up. Then I dreamt that I woke up and felt the wet cross on my left hand by applying the palm to my cheek. And then a long time afterwards I woke up really and knew at once that the hand of my physical body had been lying in a closed position undisturbed on my chest all the while.

In Type 2 false awakenings, there is an atmosphere of suspense present on "waking." The false awakening of another British writer, Oliver Fox, is typical of this type:

> 66 *I passed from unremembered dreams and thought I was awake. It was s till night and my room was very dark. Although it seemed to me that I was awake, I felt curiously disinclined to move. The atmosphere had changed, to be in a 'strained' condition. I had a sense of invisible, intangible powers at work, which caused this feeling as of aerial stress. I became expectant. Certainly something was about to happen.* 99

Type 2 false awakenings, then, are accompanied by apprehension, whereas Type 1 are not.

When the verisimilitude of the imagery with wakefulness is perfect, there will be no awareness of the false awakening, and the dreamer will drift back into an ordinary dream or into slow-wave sleep. In the morning there may a conviction of having got up for some reason during the night.

Expectation and false awakenings

A false-awakening is usually easier to induce than direct lucidity. It is produced using a powerful psychological effect -- expectation.

Dr. Hearne saw how potent expectation could be in his own sleep-laboratory experiments. In one study, subjects were wired up to his "dream machine" invention (see page 42) and additionally monitored for electrophysiological recording. They were told that they would feel four pulses to the wrist when they were dreaming (identified by the machine from their increased breathing rate) and that the pulses were to be taken as a cue for them to become lucid. For the purposes of comparison, some subjects received no pulses at all. Yet some of these reported having become lucid as a result of feeling the pulses that they were anticipating.

In another study, on memory consolidation in sleep, subjects learned material before sleep and were woken at 3am and 6am to recall the material. Dr. Hearne noticed that most of the subjects reported at 3am they had dreamed that he had woken them for a report. Again, there was an expectation — for him to appear.

The FAST technique

This technique – False Awakening with State Testing – was designed by Dr. Hearne to induce lucidity. It utilizes the power of expectation and is successful with some people. It is based on the dreamer recognizing a false-awakening and then using that halfway stage to "piggy-back" into a lucid dream or an out-of-body experience.

The first stage, then, of the FAST technique is to establish an expectation. If you want to become lucid using this method, you need an assistant who will enter your bedroom at random times throughout your sleep period. They don't have to creep in – they come in, potter around, perhaps say something to you, and then go out.

With this technique you have to develop a certain religiosity of behaviour in that whenever you think the assistant is present, no matter how certain you are that you are awake, you have to perform certain State-Testing behaviours to test whether you are definitely awake or asleep.

Sooner or later, you are going to dream, because of your expectation that the assistant is in the room. If at that point you discover by using the tests that you are, in fact, actually dreaming, you can then proceed to lucidity.

Clearly, even if you are 100 per cent sure that you are really awake, you *must* perform the tests. You may even practise the tests in the day, so that they become very familiar and routine to you.

The most important detector of dreaming is the light-switch test, which is simple enough to perform from bed, but you may dream that you are out of bed and the assistant comes in – in which case other tests may be conducted.

Here, then, is Dr. Hearne's list of ten tests for State Assessment:

1 Switch on an electric light in the dream scenery. If it does not work or there is malfunction of any kind, or a light switch cannot be found, suspect that you are dreaming. The same applies to any other electrical appliance.

2 Attempt to "float" in mid-air. Any success, of course, means that you are dreaming.

3 Jump off some sort of object. Do you descend slowly?

4 Look carefully at the surroundings. Is there anything there that should not be present or is missing?

5 Look at your body and your clothes. Is it *your* body and are the clothes yours in wakefulness?

6 Look out of a window. Is the environment accurate? Is the season correct, and is the light-level right for the time?

7 Attempt to alter a detail in the scenery, or make something happen by will-power.

8 Attempt to push your hand through solid-looking objects.

9 Pinch your skin. Are the texture and the sensation as they should be?

10 Look in a mirror. Is there some alteration to your face?

Have the attitude that the dream is out to fool you by creating very realistic situations so that you will not feel that you have to conduct the tests. Do them anyway. Often, people report that they were so convinced they were awake that they considered it foolish to perform the state tests. Only on really waking did they realize that the dreamed events did not actually happen.

Once you realize that you are dreaming, a number of options present themselves. You may simply, with the full knowledge of being in a dream body, explore the building you are in. It will seem that you will be able to walk through walls, like a ghost. In what ways is the building different from wakefulness? Who are the people in the place?

You may try to transform the condition into a typical lucid dream, by covering your dream eyes and wishing yourself, by thought, to be at a particular place. Then open your eyes and see what happens. Some people are said to achieve "astral projection," or an "out-of-body experience" (OOBE), from that state by "projecting" from their solar plexus or "forcing" their consciousness through the top of their head. If you become proficient at this technique of wishing yourself to a different location, experiment. Get someone to write a four-digit random number (preferably obtained from random number tables) on a card and place it somewhere you can "visit" in the altered state. If you are able to read the number, you will know the experiment has been successful.

CONVERTING NIGHTMARES TO LUCID DREAMS

Without realizing it, Dr. Hearne hit upon a very effective way of dealing with nightmare dreams. In October 1976 he was describing lucid dream control and his signalling technique on the radio. Shortly afterwards, a woman who had been experiencing a severe nightmare each night for many months wrote the following letter to him:

66 I listened to you on the radio on Tuesday. Until then, I had never been aware of having a lucid dream. I have vivid dreams and nightmares revolving around me lying in bed sleeping. Thus, on first awakening, it takes a little time to realize that it is only a dream and not reality. However, my last thoughts before going to sleep on Tuesday night were about the interview and I believe the result was a lucid dream. I was back in my mother-in-law's house (she died in February). Occupying most of the living room was an extra-large coffin, with the lid propped open. Four undertakers dressed in black, with long, frightening faces,

were standing by. In an equivalent situation at any other time, this is the point where I would wake up screaming, but on Tuesday there followed a completely different pattern.

Suddenly I wasn't frightened anymore. I smiled happily and distinctly remember saying, 'It is all right, it is only a dream.' I then laughingly suggested that we move the coffin lid up and down slowly to make it creak and groan. When I awoke, I recalled it all quite clearly but without fear. I felt that I must write to you because I truly believe that if I had not listened to your interview, I would have woken up screaming as usual. 99

This was a case of simple informational therapy – it works in the same way as telling sleep-paralysis sufferers to relax, rather than fight the condition. The woman's recognition at some point in the nightmare that the situation was "only a dream" defused the anxiety and terrified thoughts.

Essentially, there is a degree of logical thought going on in dreams. Most

to shrink you!' With that, the creature quickly dissolved to a furry little animal that scurried away. I felt a marvellous sense of being in control.

Another account shows a similar sense of elation at the new-found power:

I recalled what you said about controlling the dream, when I recognized the scenery that usually precedes my nightmare. With a sudden illumination of dream lucidity I decided to make the dream pleasant and soon found myself on a golden beach. I was very exhilarated.

people who report nightmares state that a thought like, "Oh my God, here's the nightmare!" nearly always precedes the episode. Because, as previously explained, what you *think* you will then *dream*, this dream-thought acts as an instruction to the imaging process.

Based on that feedback, Dr. Hearne developed a technique whereby the sufferer is encouraged to change their mind-set from, "Oh my God, here's the nightmare!" to "Great! Wonderful! Here's the nightmare. That means I'm having a lucid dream, and I can control the dream!"

Nothing can really be done for nightmares medically, but therapists report that this simple, drug-free technique is proving extremely successful for nightmare sufferers. A dramatic transformation occurs, giving the dreamer a tremendous sense of mastery:

I was being chased by something — a real monster. I suddenly realized that this was a recurring nightmare and that I could control everything. I stopped, turned round and faced the creature. I said to it, 'I'm going

Nightmare-conversion script

If you or someone you know suffers regularly from nightmares, you can employ a form of hypnotherapy to utilize the technique yourself. Following the instructions on page 79 for therapeutic techniques, use the initial relaxation script on that page followed by the nightmare-conversion script given below. Repeat this script slowly a few times, remembering to pause at the dots, then return to the pre-suggestion state as directed on page 79.

When you are asleep at night . . . and dreaming . . . and you realize . . . because you recognize the similarities . . . that the dream . . . is going to become . . . a bad dream that you have experienced before . . . instantly . . . you will become excited and happy . . . and think to yourself . . . "Great! Wonderful! I'm dreaming. This is a lucid dream!" . . . In a lucid dream you have full control over the dream. . . so you can turn and face any unwanted images that are there . . . and simply zap them . . . say, with laser beams from your fingers.. . . Then . . . with full mastery of the situation . . . you can "will" yourself to another location . . . simply by covering your dream eyes and thinking of the place where you would like to be. . . . What you think, you will then dream . . . so you can take full advantage . . . of the incredible dream world . . . to have amazing and beautiful experiences . . . so that sleep is welcomed and you think of dreams as great adventures . . . which are to be welcomed.

Regular nightmare sufferers have a great advantage over others when it comes to attaining lucidity. The awareness of dreaming is usually reached when some anomaly causes that insight, but for nightmare sufferers, the very onset of a nightmare, and its associated thought of imminent doom, is itself sufficient. All that is necessary is to alter the person's state of mind about the situation, to get them to realize that there is no need for them to worry because they are in a dream world in which the imagery can easily be manipulated to their considerable advantage. They can actually use their recognition of the onset of a previously fearful experience as a doorway into the massively exciting inner universe of the dream world.

DREAM TRACING

It is now possible to externalize the subjective, internally observed imagery of dreams induced by hypnosis, using a technique discovered by Dr. Hearne. "Oneiro" is Greek for dream, and the term *hypno-oneirography*, coined by Dr. Hearne, indicates that the method involves hypnotic dream imagery and a physical representation of the picture.

In 1954 the American hypnotherapist A. Meares got subjects simply to draw under hypnosis, as a new psychoanalytical technique which he termed hypnography. Four years later, another American hypnotherapist, C. Moss, found that she could get clients to relive a trauma on an imagined TV screen; the images could be slowed down and observed by the person. Dr. Hearne's technique is a way of accessing viewed images and producing a "print-out" of them.

The procedure is best conducted in a dimly lit or nearly dark room. The seated subject is placed in front of a large drawing board. Hypnosis is then induced in the subject, and a dream topic is suggested. At any particular point in the ongoing dream, the imagery can be stopped on the hypnotist's command – say, when a pencil is tapped on a table.

The subject is instructed to open their eyes and continue to "see" the "freeze-framed" image. A pen is placed in their hand and they then simply trace the still scene that they have "projected" on to the drawing board. Colours, textures and so on are described to the hypnotist, who makes a note of them. Afterwards, the colours may be filled in according to the subject's descriptions. The darkened room enhances the subjective "brightness" of the imagery to the subject when their eyes are open and so assists the recording of detail in the picture.

Snapshots of a dream

The old adage that "one picture is worth a thousand words" is particularly true of imagery obtained in the hypnotic state, where, often, subjects are inhibited verbally. A vast amount of information becomes available in such pictures – just as if you were looking through the eyes of the individual.

Another advantage of this method over verbal reports is that in a verbal report the subject is, through the very act of speaking, selecting what the hypnotist or therapist is told, so significant items may be missed; pictures, of course, do not have this fundamental limitation.

After the tracing is completed, the subject is told to continue with the dream until stopped for the next scene. By successively starting and stopping the dream in this way, any number of such "dream snapshots" can be acquired. The process can take a long time, but after a couple of hours, say, a whole sequence of cartoon-like glimpses of the dream will have been collected.

The scene-shift effect

When Dr. Hearne first experimented with the technique, he soon observed a consistent "scene-shift" effect. Pictures obtained before and after a scene-change show great similarities. There is no reason to doubt that the same process is involved in nocturnal dreams, so this unexpected finding provided substantial insight into the general dream-producing process.

The scene-shift effect suggests that the dream progresses along visual associative pathways, in other words, by each picture strongly influencing the structure of the following one. This is, in effect, a limitation – it is as if the dream is advancing by a "law of least effort." The pictorial elements, instead of being replaced, are simply rearranged into a new scene. The number of items and people tends to be maintained, but they are transformed into other objects or people/beings. The same colours are similarly reused. For example, in one dream tracing obtained by Dr. Hearne, which demonstrates the scene-shift effect, the first picture showed a green snake wrapped around a tree, and the next portrayed a cellar where a green pipe emerged from a wall.

Uses in therapy

Hypno-oneirography is opening the door to a new form of deep psychological understanding – especially in the area of therapy. The choice of hypnotic images is not really random – like nocturnal dreams, the images are linked to topics of interest or concern to the subject. In one case, for example, the subject produced a traced image of an old castle. It was an impressive picture, of a decaying structure, but it was clear to anyone else who looked at it that the castle was like a face and probably represented an aspect of the psychology of the hypnotized subject.

Often, the significance of blatantly symbolic scenes is not noticed at all by the subject during the hypnotic state. In some cases there may be a repression operating – in a sense, the subject does not want to comprehend the deeper meaning of the imagery viewed. It is anticipated that Dr. Hearne's tracing technique will be increasingly employed by therapists in the future.

Images from the past

When applied to the field of hypnotically induced past-life regression, where the individual is "taken back in time," startling pictures may be retrieved from apparent past lives of the patient. Apart from the historical scenery that is produced, portraits of the regressed subjects can be accessed by

getting them to find a mirror somewhere in the dream and look into it. At that point the scene is stopped and a tracing obtained.

This aspect of hypno-oneirography is especially fascinating. Are the pictures based on unconsciously observed pictures that the subject has seen during this lifetime (a phenomenon labelled cryptomnesia) or have they actually emanated from some past-life memory? To what extent are the historical details accurate? Research is clearly necessary here. It would be particularly evidential if these past-life pictures came up with information which no one living could possibly know, and which was later found to be correct.

VISIONS OF TERROR

> *A middle-aged man leant towards me, his face getting closer and closer to mine. Under his eyes, I noticed tusks sprouting from his cheeks. His teeth became distorted, his eyes grew bigger, then, resembling an animal, they mutated so that the lenses appeared like slits. He was a devilish-looking person.*

Terry Thomson, aged 55, a farmer who lives on a remote Scottish island, began experiencing terrible visions like this soon after he suffered a brain haemorrhage. To this day, very little is known

about the brain's deeper functions, which include the neurological image-making process. However, as we shall see, Terry's horrific visions bear remarkable similarities to recurring nightmares.

The brain haemorrhage

The story begins on a January evening in 1995, when, after a routine day on the farm, Terry spent an hour trying to get an old chain-saw to start. This involved a lot of strenuous activity – repeatedly pulling the starter cord. Then, while he was sawing a log, his head began to hurt. The pain rapidly grew worse. It became so severe that he began to vomit violently, and his eyes were sore to the point that he could not bear to look at anything.

When the doctor arrived, not wanting to mask important symptoms, he correctly administered a mild painkiller, then Terry was rushed to hospital. Unfortunately, however, after he had endured two days of acute pain, his symptoms were misdiagnosed as arising from the presence of a trapped nerve in his neck. Physiotherapy was prescribed, which resulted in excruciating pain during the recommended exercises. It was not until the next day that something more sinister than a trapped nerve was suspected, which resulted in Terry's being transferred to a larger hospital.

Some time later, it was discovered that he had suffered a sub-arachnoid haemorrhage in the upper left temporal area of the brain. This severe form of brain haemorrhage is usually fatal, and out of those who do survive, it is estimated that 30 per cent are left with some form of permanent damage.

The visions

At first, it is tempting to speculate that Terry's visions might have been induced partially by drugs. However, it soon became apparent that drugs had no bearing.

His first experience was quite pleasant and occurred on 1st February, when nothing more than mild painkillers had been administered:

> " *It was as if I was sitting inside a sphere, although I couldn't see myself. I saw patterns which began to develop slowly; at first, they were simple in appearance. My first thought was, 'Am I in this sphere because I'm ill?' Because once before when I was ill, I found myself in a sphere with beautiful, long grass growing.*

I opened my eyes (in real life), and, apart from seeing things as if through a crystal ball, everything was normal. The moment I closed them, patterns began to form again, only this time they took on fantastic shapes and colours. I remember thinking that if only I could paint them, I'd earn a fortune; they were like nothing I'd ever seen before, nor could find the words to describe — they were new colours and shapes.

The patterns made up the walls of the sphere and were a mixture of different-textured surfaces, some like fabric. They blended into each other to produce even more complex shapes and colours. Then the sphere began to rotate, and it got even more spectacular. It sped up, then slowed down. The faster it went, the darker the colours became. As it slowed down, the opposite effect was achieved. Different designs were merging into such complex and varied shapes at such speed that I was unable to recall a single thing in detail — it was too much to take in.

All the time, I knew I was conscious, because if I opened my eyes, I saw everything as it should be, with the exception that everything still appeared as though I was gazing through a crystal ball. On one occasion, when I closed my eyes, I floated into the velvety blackness of space, the complex patterns travelling by me at speed. I travelled farther in space than my mind could comprehend. ""

Research into this case has brought to light certain elements that could be responsible for such visions. The massive blood loss that took place would have exerted pressure in and around various parts of the brain. Indeed, there is more than one area of this complex organ that is given to producing different kinds of imagery. For example, dreams, day-dreams, hallucinations and conventional waking vision, to name a few, all stimulate different nerves.

During Terry's stay in hospital, the visions continued, but were soon to take on a far more sinister nature. They became so terrifying that, due to genuine concern about being regarded as mentally unstable, he soon became unwilling to mention them to the staff; only close family members were aware of his dreadful plight. The visions grew more alarming by degrees, although from the outset they struck fear into his heart.

To return to the first paragraph of Terry's account (page 106), just before the middle-aged man in the vision began to mutate, several people who were friendly in appearance had gathered around his bedside. The description continues as follows:

"" *All of them mutated until their features were hideous. I was so frightened that I opened my eyes to find them gone! However, when I closed them again, I discovered even more people, and the whole process was repeated. There*

was nothing I could do to prevent them from becoming grotesque, and this went on for several hours. It reached the stage when, despite the pain of seeing reality, I was too frightened to close my eyes. ""

Terry's next experience was even more terrifying:

"" *People gathered around my bedside again. They were happy and smiling and seemed pleased to see me. This time I decided that I wasn't going to be frightened, I would face up to it, and so decided to keep my eyes closed.*

As they got closer, they mutated again and their heads became enlarged. At the same time, I could feel myself getting smaller. I continued to shrink until I was the size of a small particle. Then I entered one of their animal-like eyes. I felt that it was because I had decided not to be frightened. As I entered the socket, I was full of wonderment while being frightened and fascinated at the same time. It felt as if I was being shown this as a sort of progression.

Inside the head, there was a huge dance hall which was full of people. I focused on one particular couple, but they also began to mutate.

I opened my eyes. They were gone and I was seeing the hospital ward again. The moment I closed them, they came again, mutating as they approached. I entered another eye to see another dance hall. This time, however, there was elaborate scenery and a mixture of different people who, in turn, mutated. I entered one of their eyes, only to see yet another dance hall, with even more people changing into the most hideous creatures. ""

Two years after his haemorrhage, Terry still experienced these visions, although they were less frightening. They usually occurred when he felt at a low ebb — for example, when he had a cold, the flu or a slight temperature. Upon retiring for the night, the moment he closed his eyes he saw a variety of people (sometimes in profile only), who approached him and appeared to take a keen interest in him.

The possible causes

When David Melbourne heard about Terry's plight, he began researching the possible causes — such as pressure on nerves, blood clots or scarring, but was unable to find anything that would account categorically for the recurring nature or the type of visions experienced.

If Terry had been on powerful cocaine-based drugs, for instance, he might have imagined that bugs had burrowed under his skin — these are commonly referred to as cocaine bugs. Other drugs are known to produce various specific images and sensations, but none conform to Terry's experience or circumstances, which rules them out. Petit mal, a mild form of epilepsy which also induces vision-like phenomena, was also excluded.

It has been discovered that by repeatedly stimulating designated areas of the brain, the same memories can be made to reappear. Therefore, stretching the imagination, the possibility exists that in Terry's case the same nerve cells might have been triggered in a repetitive sequence, but it still does not answer the question of what caused the horrific visions.

The similarity to nightmares

According to Melbourne's own research, however, a consistent link or bridge between the subconscious and conscious awareness is possible. In Terry's case, it happened by accident (the haemorrhage), but similar evidence can be found in psychics, some of whom see visions. A good example is the premonitions that may be seen during the transitional interval between consciousness and sleep, sometimes known as the "hypnagogic bridge." Meditation techniques have enabled some individuals to extend this period considerably, and it was under these circumstances that Barbara Garwell foresaw the attempted assassination of the Pope (see page 46).

The fact that such visions bear a resemblance to the characteristics of recurring nightmares raises many unanswered questions. It was precisely this feature that made Melbourne consider whether both phenomena could be related.

As we have seen on pages 71–2, Melbourne's own work in the field of dreams indicates that nightmares often serve the purpose of alerting us to something that our subconscious has identified as needing some thought; and the bad dreams may recur until the root cause registers in the conscious mind, at which point they frequently cease.

The fact that Terry's visions persisted can be explained in terms of science, but what was the reason for the recurring theme? Although it is reasonable to assume that the damaged nerves might be the same nerves which, from time to time, are fired to produce the visions, that still does not account for their specific nature.

The interpretation

However, if we approach the problem from a different angle – that of a dream analyst – then things could begin to make some sense. Because Melbourne recognized that Terry's visions bore a striking resemblance to the images of recurring nightmares, he set about analysing them accordingly.

Terry had always trusted the medical profession, but when his brain haemorrhage was misdiagnosed as a mere trapped nerve, he began to have grave misgivings. Even worse, the prescribed treatment – a gruelling programme of physiotherapy – only made an already painful condition more agonizing.

Terry's doubts began to harden into unadulterated mistrust. Instinctively, he *knew* how ill he was – something had to be radically wrong with him – so

why couldn't these experts see it? By the time Terry had the emergency transfer to another hospital, his confidence in the medical profession had been all but shattered. Even later, long after he had been discharged from hospital, he found that he still harboured serious reservations during his visits as an out-patient.

These circumstances matched the pattern of Terry's visions so well that they almost analysed themselves. Nevertheless, Melbourne had to be sure and so embarked on the long road of interpretation. Almost immediately, though, he had little doubt as to the cause of Terry's visions. The images of people approaching his hospital bed matched the various staff members who would come to see him.

In dream analysis, when somebody's features change or "mutate," as Terry described it, this can, on occasion, be suggesting that they are in some way two-faced, or are not who they claim to be. The latter interpretation fitted neatly into the general analysis.

The horrific nature of the individuals in the visions reflected the horrendous ordeal that Terry was put through. Then, when he ventured through the eye sockets (desperately trying to get through to these people, or get inside their heads), he was faced with more of the same (other staff who, it seemed, were not who they claimed to be). In truth, he was seeing them as ogres, who were almost experimenting on him. This even fitted with the environment or dance hall to which the visions had progressed (leading him a merry dance).

As the subsequent weeks of his convalescence grew into months, so the visions became less fearful, but he still witnessed people gathering around him. Again, this reflected the circumstances perfectly. These characters were still indicative of the medical profession, but perhaps less responsible for Terry's trauma. In other words, they matched unequivocally the situation of visiting the out-patients' department.

If Melbourne's theory was correct, he had pinpointed the root cause of Terry's visions. When

Melbourne made his findings known to Terry, he identified with them immediately – it all made wonderful sense to him.

The recovery

Melbourne knew that if he was right, the next time Terry was under the weather and experienced visions something quite special would happen. Less than two months later, Terry informed Melbourne that he had been ill for a few days, during which time he experienced some visions. As before, people approached him, but this time they were uninterested. However, there followed a remarkable episode, one which marked the end of their horrific nature. The last person he saw approach him and look into his eyes was Jean, his wife. This had never happened before, and it preceded the most impressive visions set in spectacular surroundings.

In one instance, he floated up into space where he was shown various intricacies – though he cannot recall now what they were. During another vision, he found himself suspended about 15 metres (50 feet) above fantastic scenery. The sky was deep blue and the air was clean and warm around his body. Then he began to rise up, until finally he was looking down at the earth as a globe. Terry described it as a wondrous scene.

At the time of writing, Terry underwent another episode, and one that marked the end of the horrific nature of the visions, for good. He reported that the faces of strangers which used to gather round him were no longer able to materialize. They appeared as if without substance, then evaporated!

REVERSE SPEECH AND DREAM INTERPRETATION

Another intriguing new area of research, which could be very important for dream research, is that of reverse speech. In 1991, the Australian David Oates,

based in the United States, reported an amazing discovery which seems to show the operation of the unconscious in ordinary speech. He found that if speech is recorded and then played backwards, distinct words, phrases and whole sentences can sometimes be heard. These reverse speech utterances appear not to be random but are related to the subject matter of the forward speech (known as complementarity). The brain is complex and, it appears, can analyse speech in both directions.

The unconscious cleverly influences the selection of spoken words so that both a forward and a backward message can occasionally (perhaps every ten seconds or so) be produced. For example, Neil Armstrong's famous words, "That's one small step for man . . . ," when reversed, clearly say, "Man will spacewalk."

It is fascinating to consider that while two people converse consciously, their unconscious minds are also communicating. This could explain much of the "intuition" we have about people. The unconscious communication is straightforward and honest, revealing the real attitude of the individual.

Dr. Hearne and David Melbourne have begun to research this phenomenon in relation to dreams. One dream report by a 74-year-old woman described an anxiety dream about her son. Reversing her account, the words "Help me, somebody" and "I'll survive" were heard. This is, potentially, an enormously important area in psychology and could reveal much about unconscious processes.

OUR PERSPECTIVE TODAY

To sum up, the perspective we now have on dreams is rather complex. The existence of two types of sleep, SWS and REM sleep, is a fairly recent discovery. REM sleep itself is the matrix in which dreams are embedded, but while it seemed at one time that there was an absolute necessity to dream, that notion does not now fit the facts. As we have seen, dreaming sleep

may be abolished by certain drugs over the long-term with no massive and accumulating harmful effects.

The likelihood is that REM sleep and dreams are significant in the foetus or the newborn baby. A baby does not suddenly become conscious at birth – it is sentient within the womb – and it may be that innate imagery of some kind is actually "played" to the foetus. Some theories have sought to explain REM sleep rather than dreams, but we have also observed that some of these proposals have simply reflected the current technological vogues. Essentially, we are still not certain about the function of REM sleep.

From this vantage point, we can also see that the various dream theories in the last 150 years or so have generally contributed something to our understanding of dreams, but their narrowness of application has inevitably resulted in their decline. In particular, the Freudian doctrine – though greatly influential and compelling for a while – has necessarily fallen in support.

The latest approach to dream interpretation, particularly that of the authors, has reverted to the ancient Roman procedure of looking at dreams logically and systematically (though obviously with the benefit of modern insights) without imposing any one theory on the reported dream material.

The recent development of studying dream lucidity has opened up the dream world to systematic investigation – from within. The discovery of the universal "light-switch effect" – whereby the light level in a dream cannot be increased, making it impossible to switch on a light in a dream – was significant in revealing the limitations the dream-producing process has to contend with.

The "rules" of imagery production have been further disclosed through the study of hypnotic dreams. The method of hypno-oneirography, in which "freeze-framed" pictures are projected on to a surface and physically traced, revealed the "scene-shift effect," whereby the visual elements of a scene are simply rearranged into the next scene. More phenomena consistent with this are likely to be found.

Thus, as we have seen, the dream clearly flows along verbal and visual associative pathways, representing thoughts in visual symbolic form, rather than distorting the thoughts in order to disguise them. It functions economically, almost by a "law of least effort," and is forced to operate within various natural limitations of imagery-construction – it makes do with the current situation.

THE FUTURE

Looking ahead a few decades, it is apparent that the technical revolution that is already building up momentum will take over our dreaming along with the rest of our lives. This, combined with widespread use of lucid dreaming, will help to develop what is essentially a new frontier: the inner universe.

Dream machines

Electronic "dream machines," developed from Dr. Hearne's original invention – which used pulses to the wrist to alert the dreamer that they were dreaming, to enable them to become lucid – will probably become commonplace in the future. These will help people to access their inner dream universe – either to recall more dreams or to induce lucidity experimentally.

Various experiments will doubtless be conducted between geographically distant dreamers with such devices. It is possible that when a dream machine linked to one dreamer detects dreaming sleep, the device could automatically link (using, say, the Internet) with someone else's device, to determine if that person was also dreaming. If so, external-stimuli pulses could be administered to both persons in order to initiate lucidity, without waking. Under those circumstances, would interesting similarities occur in their dreams?

Lucid dreaming

As we have seen, lucid dreams hold a limitless potential. They can enhance the quality of life for people in so many areas. Once dream awareness and control are attained, the simple recreational aspect can be utilized fully, whether the dreamer wishes to soar through the air, visit exotic new locations or meet interesting people. The state of lucidity is also ideal for self-exploration and realizing one's potential. A major development will be the use of such dreams for the early medical detection of illness and for healing. The potent innovational features of the lucid dream will be increasingly exploited too by artists, writers, composers, architects, film-makers and anyone seeking an original concept.

Tuning in to dreams

It seems likely that sensing devices will be developed to a high state, enabling the brain to be minutely monitored from instrumentation placed near the scalp. Incredible, perhaps frightening, advances might then ensue, including being able to "tune in" to dreams as they occur. We might be able literally to see on a television screen what people are dreaming. Privacy will then have disappeared – it will be possible to tap into thoughts and dreams. It is predicted that a first stage in this process will be the detection of sounds within dreams.

People will be able to record their dreams, play them back and show others. At that time, the dream's secrets will have been laid bare and the age-old mystery of what they are about will be solved. It will be possible to analyse them, frame by frame.

Virtual reality

Dreams will also be associated with virtual reality. VR, as it is known, is going to be the biggest revolution in the history of the world – and yet it is only a few decades away. Forget the helmet devices that are the current state of the art. Fairly soon, we shall probably have VR contact lenses, each linked remotely to a small but phenomenal computer system. The lenses will modify visual input and create imagery, the quality of which will make it indistinguishable from "real" vision.

In VR, everyone will look and sound beautiful. Our real environment will be absolutely minimalistic, because our lenses will create the most exquisite surroundings. People will probably interact less and less, because computer-generated friends will be much more interesting and totally caring.

Our dreams, recorded from our brains, will be fed into VR systems. Thus, a person you dreamed of could be presented, as real as life, in wakefulness through the VR system. Someone you met in a dream could even become a life-long companion, generated by the computer.

In a few decades most people will probably be spending all their wakefulness in virtual reality. We are, actually, the last to experience cold, harsh natural reality.

In a few years' time, the meaning of reality is going to change from the way we understand it. The evolution to this state of affairs is absolutely unstoppable.

Will this be the ultimate, wonderful dream — or will it turn out to be the worst nightmare imaginable? The authors are optimistic, believing that people's lives will be made incredibly more worthwhile and vastly enriched, while their spiritual progress will be assisted greatly by the infinite variety of their experiences.

Dreams are a part of all our lives, often reflecting our deepest emotions and most profound experiences, yet they generally seem ambiguous, perplexing and veiled in mystery. Exploring your dreams can take you on a journey of self-discovery. If you feel that a particular dream is significant – say, because of its vividness and your strength of feeling on waking – you may wish to look much deeper into its hidden meaning. Three different ways of doing this are described here. All three  methods are designed to help you penetrate deeper into the maze of your unconscious and the extraordinary world of your dreams.

Each method of exploring your dreams involves the cooperation of someone whom you trust and who is impartial concerning what happens in your life. That person should not be emotionally close to you or likely to feature in the dream.

For the three methods covered here, you and the person helping you will both need adequate background information. You therefore must prepare beforehand a full, written (preferably word-processed) account of the dream, and also describe the dream in detail to the person who will be helping you.

When attempting any of these methods, be sure to turn off the phone and go through the procedure at a time when you will not be disturbed.

THE IMR METHOD

An IMR, or Ideo Motor Response, is a means of getting simple Yes/No answers from the unconscious by means of slight and unnoticed muscular twitches (in this case, of the fingers) in response to questions. By circumventing the defences and biases of consciousness, truer answers should be attained. The method is probing for answers concerning the different elements of the dream, in order to gain as much insight as possible.

The actual procedure for obtaining the answers to the questions is described under "Procedure" (see page 121).

Broad topic of dream
First you will establish the broad topic of the dream. To do this, ask the following questions:

- **Is the dream mainly about . . .**
  a present situation?
  a past situation?
  a situation that will or may arise?
  a problem?
  something good?
  health?

employment?
family?
friends?
a relationship?
- **Is the dream a premonition?**
- **Is the dream urging you to take a course of action?**

Add other topics you think might be relevant, and narrow down the area by appropriate questioning.

List of elements

Based on the dream account, you and your associate need to construct a list of the dream's elements. In making the list, use the exact descriptive words from the dream account. Include all the types of element shown in the following list.

TYPE OF ELEMENT	EXAMPLES OF ELEMENTS
• **Person**	*The man with glasses, "Susie"*
• **Creature**	*The Persian cat, the frog, the puppies*
• **Building**	*The house you were in, the shop you saw, the tower you noticed*
• **Location**	*The mountains, the garden, the ocean*
• **Item**	*The figurine, the car, the bottle*
• **Activity**	*Ploughing, running away, cooking*
• **Event**	*The torrent of water, the avalanche, the parade*
• **Other observation**	*The bullet holes in your body, the paint peeling off the wall, the smell of pine cones*

List of questions

Now, for each of the dream elements in your list, draw up a series of unambiguous questions to which the answer will be either Yes or No. Your collaborator may well come up with questions that your unconscious would rather avoid, so that person's input here is essential.

The general format should be, "*Does [A] represent [B]?*" The elements will be substituted, one by one, for [A] in this formula. For [B] you need to make a list of possibilities appropriate to each element.

For example, under the People category, if you had listed "the man with glasses" as an element, these would be typical questions you would ask: Does the man with glasses represent himself? Does the man with glasses represent you? Does the man with glasses represent your partner?

Once you had asked all the questions about the man with glasses, you would move on to the next element – in the examples above, it is "Susie" – and once again go through the series of questions. The same applies to all the other elements. Try to narrow down the selection as much as possible. Possible questions for each type of element are as follows:

Person Does he or she represent . . . you? your partner? a family member? a friend? a work colleague? someone you have met recently? a person under 25? a person 25 or older? a metaphor (e.g. a worker, a layabout)? a problem? something good?

Creature Does it represent . . . itself? a person (if Yes, go to People list)? a metaphor (e.g. a dog, a pig, a lion, a busy bee)? a problem? something good?

Building Does it represent . . . a building you have seen? your home? your body? a person (if Yes, go to People list)? a metaphor (e.g. a church symbolizing spirituality or a wedding)? a problem? something good?

Location Does it represent . . . a place you have seen? a metaphor (e.g. all at sea, up the creek, in the hot spot)? a problem? something good?

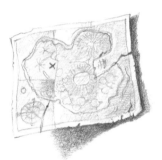

Item Does it represent . . . itself? a part of your body? a metaphor (e.g. an iron could represent sorting or smoothing things out)? a problem? something good?

Activity Does it represent . . . itself? a metaphor (e.g. ploughing could represent doing heavy work or having sex)? a problem? something good?

Event Does it represent . . . itself? a metaphor (e.g. a torrent of water might refer to strong emotions; an avalanche might mean an inundation of work)? a problem? something good?

Other observation Does it represent . . . itself? a metaphor (e.g. bullet holes in the body might refer to emotional hurt that has occurred)? a problem? something good?

Remember that verbal puns happen a lot in dreams. You can check them by asking directly whether, perhaps, the wisteria represents hysteria, the reef means a wreath, or Mary means marry. Eventually, you will have a long list of straightforward questions to be asked by your associate.

Procedure

1 First select a "Yes" finger (say, right index) and a "No" finger (say, left index) – use whichever seem appropriate for you. You may, if you wish, also train a "Don't Know" finger. Note: If you are skilled at using a pendulum for Yes/No responses, you may use that method instead.

2 Next, train your fingers. Sitting comfortably at a table, with your eyes closed, rest your hands flat on the table, with the two response fingers raised a few centimetres (an inch or so) above the surface. Get your associate to ask you about ten questions to which the answer will clearly be Yes, and the same number that will elicit a No response. The two types of question should be presented in a random order. In this training session, simply make a conscious, but slight, lifting movement of the correct finger for each question. Examples of the type of question to practise on are: Are you male? Do you live in a house? Is your partner called Ivan? Are you from Tibet? Is your skin green?

3 Before actually beginning, sit quietly for a few minutes with your eyes closed and enter a state of relaxation. The initial relaxation script on page 79 or a suitable tape would help.

4 When you are relaxed, your associate should ask each of the prepared questions (see below) slowly and deliberately. *Do not make conscious finger signals.* You may think that nothing is happening, but sit it through. If genuine, an IMR is a *very slight twitch*, which will not be noticed by you.

Your associate must look very closely at your fingers to look for the small responses. An IMR may take several seconds to appear, so there must be a long pause between questions. Your collaborator will need to tick the Yes or No response to each of the prepared questions. Other questions may be noted down and included by the associate at the time, if the signalled answers indicate an avenue to explore.

5   After the session, take time to come back to normal alertness and then inspect the answers. They may amaze you – be prepared for revelations! You may wish to plan a further investigation of the dream, based on all the information that was acquired.

THE BRIDGE METHOD

Another technique for delving into a dream is to recall it then to focus on any emotions, bodily sensations and key words or phrases, in order to rekindle any previous life experiences that could be significant factors. (In therapy, a "bridge method" provides a way of linking a person's present psychological state with that of the past.) This method was devised by the American therapists John Watkins in 1971 and Morris Netherton in 1978.

Again, it is best to work with a trusted, impartial person, and a detailed written account of the dream is a necessary starting point. Full notes should be taken of the proceedings by the person helping you.

Procedure

1 Make a list of the following aspects of the dream, writing down the exact description that appears in the account of the dream:

- Any strong emotions encountered in the dream, and the events occurring then

- Any bodily sensations and the part of the body affected
- Any key words or phrases

2 Next, sit quietly for a few minutes with your eyes closed, and enter a state of relaxation – again, the initial relaxation script on page 79 or a suitable tape would help.

3 When you believe you are suitably relaxed, the person who is helping you goes through the list, and slowly says the words which are shown below for each of the various items on the list. The person should use the exact description for each one, and should pause where the dots are shown in the scripts given below.

Emotions

"Focus on the dream and the particular emotion [restating the words of the dream account connected with the emotion]. . . . Allow yourself to become immersed in that scenario. . . . Recall a previous time you felt that way."

Unexpectedly, you may find yourself suddenly in a previous event in this life (or even an apparent past life) that you have forgotten. On introspection, definite associations may be discovered between the earlier event and the dream – useful information to help in its understanding.

Bodily sensations

"Focus on that physical sensation and the dream events at the time. . . . Allow yourself to be engrossed in what is happening . . . If that [describe the sensation using the dreamer's exact words, e.g., "funny tingling in my head"] could speak, what is the first thing it would say?"

You may find that interesting, novel thoughts come into your head. Say them aloud. There may be a link between them and the dream.

Key words and phrases

"Focus on the dream, now. Repeat to me this [word/phrase] *several times and then let me know if it stirs any memories or thoughts."*

The situation of repeating the words may trigger deeper, forgotten links to things from the past that are relevant to the dream.

THE EMPTY CHAIR METHOD

Pioneered by the psychologist Fritz Perls in America in the early 1950s, this method best involves placing two chairs facing each other, but about a metre (a few feet) apart. When you sit in one chair, you enact the role of *you* – the person who had the dream. When you sit in the other chair, you enact the role of the *dream character* you wish to talk with.

As *you*, ask a question to any of the characters you saw in the dream. Then physically move to the other chair, sit in it and come up with a response.

Using pure imagination and saying whatever comes into your head, you may find that hidden truths begin to emerge from this little game.

Despite the spontaneous nature of this method, you do still need to write down a full account of the dream beforehand, and to select in advance the characters you wish to question. Once again, you will

need someone to help you, as they should make full notes during the dialogue, so that you can carefully analyse what was said afterwards.

LUCID DREAM EXPERIMENTS

If you experience lucid dreams, in which you become fully aware of being in a dream – as though you were conscious – and can, by thought, control the dream's activities, you may like to assist with some important research by conducting one or more experiments *within the lucid dream state* and reporting to us what happened.

Here is the list of experiments. Select as many as you like and please provide a clear, detailed written or typed account of the results. Please make it clear which experiment you conduct by stating the letter and number (for example, A-3: mirror experiment).

For each experiment, please report whether the dream imagery was VERY VIVID, DIM, or IN BETWEEN.

A YOUR BODY IN THE DREAM:
1 Look at your hands. Are they different from reality?
2 Look at other parts of your body. Are they different?
3 Find a mirror and look into it. Is your face different?

B GRAVITY IN DREAMS:
1 Jump off, say, a chair. What happens?
2 Throw an object. How does it fall to the ground?
3 Drop an object. How does it fall to the ground?

C ELECTRICAL ITEMS:
1 Switch on a light. What happens?
2 Switch a light off, then on again. What happens?
3 Switch on an electrical appliance. What happens?

D HEALTH:
1 In the lucid dream, visit someone you know who is ill and attempt healing by visualizing white light around them. What happens in the dream scenery? Did the person subsequently appear to improve in reality?
2 Visit a dream doctor and have a medical check-up. What happens?

E SCENE CHANGES:
1 Carefully observe a scene, then change it to something else. On waking, draw a picture of each of those scenes.

F COLOURS:
1 Change the colour of an object several times. Report.

G LOCATION CHANGING:
1 "Cover" your (dream) eyes and think the name of a place where you would like to be. On waking, draw pictures of the "before" and "after" scenes.

H THE SENSES:
1 Look at some print. Report.
2 Clap your hands together suddenly. Does the sound reach your ears immediately?
3 Taste a food. Is it the same as in wakefulness?
4 Smell a food or scented object. Is it the same as in wakefulness?
5 Pinch your skin. Does it feel the same as in wakefulness?

I THE NIGHT SKY:
1 If you find yourself in a "night" dream, where you can see the stars, planets and moon, note carefully the position of those objects and draw their relative positions on waking. If you are familiar with astronomy, give any comments.

J MATTER PENETRATION:
1 Try moving your hand through objects made of different materials. Report.

When you send your information, please answer these questions:

● How frequently (on average) do you have lucid dreams?
● How old were you when you started to have lucid dreams?
● What usually makes you aware of being in a dream?
● Have you noticed any unusual, consistent effects in your dreams? If so, please give details.

Please also supply the following:
● Name and address
● Date, place and time of birth

We cannot promise to respond to each report sent in, but all the data will be carefully read, collated and analysed.

Please send your report to us at
42 Borden Avenue, Enfield, Middlesex ENI 2BY, England

BIBLIOGRAPHY

Adler, A. (1958) *What Life Should Mean to You.* Capricorn, New York.

Artemidorus In White, R.

Aserinsky, E. & Kleitman, N. (1953) Regular periods of eye motility and concomitant phenomena during sleep. *Science,* 118, 273–4.

Aubrey, J. (1890; orig. 1696) *Miscellanies.* Library of Old Authors, Reeves & Turner, London.

Berger, H. (1929) Über das Elektenkephalogramm des Menschen. *Archiv für Psychiatrie und Nervenkrankheiten.* 87, 527–70.

Binz (1878) In Freud, S.

Caton, R. (1875) The electric currents of the brain. *British Medical Journal.* 2, 278.

Cattell, R. & Eber, J. (1969) *Sixteen Personality Factor Questionnaire.* Institute for Personality and Ability Testing, Illinois.

Crick, F. & Mitchison, G. (1986) REM sleep and neural nets. *The Journal of Mind and Behaviour,* Spring–Summer.

de Becker, R. (1968) *The Understanding of Dreams, or the Machinations of the Night.* George Allen and Unwin, London.

Delage, Y. (1891) In Freud, S.

Delboeuf (1885) In Freud, S.

Dodds, E.R. (1971) Supernormal phenomena in classical antiquity. *Proceedings of the Society for Psychical Research,* 55 (205), 189–237.

Evans, C. & Newman, E.

(1964) Dreaming: an analogy from computers. *New Scientist,* 24, 577–9.

Evans-Wentz, W. (1960) *The Tibetan Book of the Dead.* Oxford University Press, Oxford.

Eysenck, H. (1953) *Uses and Abuses of Psychology.* Penguin, London.

Faraday, A. (1972) *Dream Power.* Hodder & Stoughton, London.

Faraday, A. (1974) *The Dream Game.* Hodder & Stoughton, London.

Fisher, C., Byrne, J., & Edwards, A. (1968) NREM and REM nightmares. *Psychobiology.* 5: 22–222.

Fontana, D. (1993) *The Secret Language of Symbols.* Pavilion Books, London.

Fordham, F. (1953) *An Introduction to Jung's Psychology.* Pelican Books, London.

Fox, O. (1962) *Astral Projection.* University Books Inc., New York.

Frazer, J. (1994; orig.1890) *The Golden Bough. A History of Myth and Religion.* Chancellor Press, London.

Freud, S. (1961; orig. 1900) *The Interpretation of Dreams.* George Allen and Unwin, London.

Garfield, P. (1974) *Creative Dreaming.* Ballantine Books, New York.

Garwell, B. (1996) *Dreams that Come True.* Thorsons, Wellingborough.

Graham, H. (1995) *A Picture of Health.* Piatkus Books, London.

Green, C. (1968) *Lucid Dreams.* Institute for Psychophysical Research, Oxford.

Gurney, E., Myers, F. & Podmore, F. (1918) *Phantasms of the Living.* Kegan Paul, Trench, Trubner & Co., London.

Hahn, E., Dement, C., Fisher, C. & Barmcak, J. (1962) Incidence in colour immediately recalled dream. *Science,* 137: 1055–6.

Hall, C. (1953) *The Meaning of Dreams.* Harper and Row, New York.

Hearne, K. (1973) *Some Investigations into Hypnotic Dreams Using a New Technique.* B.Sc. project, Dept. of Psychology, University of Reading.

Hearne, K. (1975) *Visual Imagery and Evoked Responses.* M.Sc. thesis, Dept. of Psychology, University of Hull.

Hearne, K. (1978) *Lucid Dreams – an Electrophysiological and Psychological Study.* Ph.D. thesis, Dept. of Psychology, University of Liverpool.

Hearne, K. (1981) A light-switch phenomenon in lucid dreams. *Journal of Mental Imagery,* 5 (2), 97–100.

Hearne, K. (1981) Lucid dreams and ESP. *Journal of the Society for Psychical Research,* 51 (787), 7–11.

Hearne, K. (1982) Effects of performing certain set tasks in the lucid dream state. *Perceptual and Motor Skills,* 54, 259–62.

Hearne, K. (1984) Lucid dreams and psi research.

Current trends in Psi Research – Proceedings of an International Conference held in New Orleans, Louisiana, August 13–14. Eds. B. Shapiro & L. Coly, Parapsychology Foundation, Inc., New York, 192–218.

Hearne, K. (1986) An analysis of premonitions deposited over one year, from an apparently gifted subject. *Journal of the Society for Psychical Research,* 53 (804), 376–82.

Hearne, K. (1987) A new perspective in dream imagery. *Journal of Mental Imagery,* 11 (2), 75–82.

Hearne, K. (1989) *Visions of the Future.* The Aquarian Press, Wellingborough.

Hearne, K. (1990) *The Dream Machine.* The Aquarian Press, Wellingborough.

Hildebrandt (1875) In Freud, S.

Jessen (1855) In Freud, S.

Jones, E. (1949) *On the Nightmare.* Hogarth Press, London.

Jouvet, M. (1975) The function of dreaming: A neurophysiologist's point of view. *Handbook of Psychobiology.* Eds. Gazzaniga, M. and Blakemore, C. Academic Books, N.Y.

Jung, C. (1964) *Man and His Symbols.* Aldus Books, London.

Karacan, J., Goodenough, R., & Shapiro, S. (1966) Erection cycle during sleep in relation to dream anxiety. *Archives of General Psychiatry,* 15: 183–9.

LaBerge, S. (1980) *Lucid dreaming: an exploratory study of consciousness during sleep.* Unpublished Ph.D thesis, Stanford University, California.

Maury, A. (1878) In Freud, S.

McCurdy, H. (1946) The history of dream theory. *Psychological Review*, 53: 225–33.

McKellar, P. (1957) *Imagination and Thinking.* Cohen and West, London.

McKenzie, N. (1965) *Dreams and Dreaming.* Aldus Books, London.

Meares, A. (1954) Hypnography – a technique in hypnoanalysis. *Journal of Mental Science.* 100: 965–74.

Mégroz, R. (1939) *The Dream World.* John Lane, The Bodley Press, London.

Melbourne, D. & Hearne, K.

(1997) *Dream Interpretation—the Secret.* Blandford Press, London.

Melbourne, D. & Hearne, K. (1997) *The Melbourne/Hearne Questionnaire* (MHQ). Available from the authors.

Moss, C. (1958) Dream symbols as disguises. *ETC.* 14: 267–73.

Oates, D. (1991) *Reverse Speech: Hidden Messages in Human Communication.* Knowledge Systems, Inc.

Peek, P. (1991) *African Divinatory Systems – Ways of Knowing.* Indiana University Press, Indiana.

Popper, K. (1959) *The Logic of Scientific Discovery.* Basic Books, New York.

Price, H. (1949) Psychical research and human personality. *The Hibbert Journal,* 47, 105–13.

Robert (1886) In Freud, S.

St Denys, Hervey de (1982; orig. 1867) *Dreams and How to Guide Them.* Trans. Nicholas Fry, ed. M. Schatzman, Duckworth, London.

Sauneron, S. (1959) *Les songes et leur interprétation dans l'Égypte ancienne.* Paris.

Scherner, A. (1861) In Freud, S.

Schleiermacher (1862) In Freud, S.

Spence, L. (No date) *The Magic and Mysteries of Mexico.* Rider & Co.

Spitta (1892) In Freud, S.

Strumpell, L. (1877) In Freud, S.

Time-Life Books (1990) *Dreams and Dreaming and Psychic Voyages (Mysteries of the Unknown).* The Time Inc. Book Company,

Alexandria, Virginia.

Ullman, M. (1958) Dreams and the therapeutic process. *Psychiatry.* 21: 123–131.

Ullman, M., Krippner, S., & Vaughan, A. (1973) *Dream Telepathy.* MacMillan, New York.

Van Eeden, F. (1913) A study of dreams. *Proceedings of the Society for Psychical Research,* XXVI (LXVII), 431–61.

White, R. (1975) *The Interpretation of Dreams* (translation of *Oneirocritica* by Artemidorus). Noyes Press, Park Ridge, New Jersey.

Williams, R., Karacan, I. & Hursch, C. (1974) *Electroencephalography of Human Sleep: Clinical Applications.* Wiley, New York.

Wundt (1880) In Freud, S.

RESOURCES

American Sleep Disorders Association
1610 14th St NW, Suite 300,
Rochester, MN 55901, USA
Tel. 507-287 6006

National Sleep Foundation
729 15th St NW, 4th floor,
Washington, DC 20005, USA

Narcolepsy Association UK
1 Brook St,
Stoke-on-Trent, ST4 1JN,
England
Tel. 01273-832725

Narcolepsy Network
PO Box 1365, FDR Station,
New York, NY 10150 USA
Tel. 914-834 2855

The Society for Psychical Research
49 Marloes Rd,
London W8 6LA, England

Helen Wozniak
42 Borden Ave,
Enfield EN1 2BY, England
Tel. 0181-372 3124

(Sleep and dream disorders therapy)

ACKNOWLEDGEMENTS

The publisher would like to thank the following sources for their kind permission to reproduce the photographs in this book:

Jacket: Image Bank, Images Colour Library

Archiv für Kunst und Geschichte 14 left and right, 20, 26-7, 31 right

Bridgeman Art Library /British Museum 12 /Museo Nazionale di Capodimonte 16 left

e t Archive 21, 22-3, 23

Freud Museum 29 right

Hulton Picture Library 48 inset

Images Colour Library 2, 4, 13, 14-15, 15, 16-17, 18, 19, 22 left, 25, 30-1, 34-5, 59, 83, 116, 117

Kobal Collection 105

Rex Features 36-7, 68-9, 92

Science Photo Library 28-29

INDEX